The hand made
GREENHOUSE
from windowsill to backyard

DATE DUE

The hand made
GREENHOUSE
from windowsill to backyard

By Richard Nicholls

Running Press, Philadelphia, Pennsylvania

Printed in the United States of America

Distributed in Canada by Van Nostrand Reinhold Ltd., Ontario

Library of Congress Catalog Card Number 74-31541

ISBN 0-914 294-12-1

Book Concept:
Diane Denbo Stevens

Illustrations of accessories in chapters 10 & 11 courtesy
of Lord & Burnham

Art Direction and Illustration: Jim Wilson
Cover Illustration: Amy Myers
Design & Graphics: Tom Fetterman
Type: Helvetica Light, Composition by Alpha Publications, Inc.

This book may be ordered directly from the publisher. Please include 25¢ postage.

Try your bookstore first.

Running Press, 38 South Nineteenth Street, Philadelphia, Pennsylvania 19103

CONTENTS

PREMISE

This is a book about greenhouses. While its primary purpose is to assist readers who wish to construct their own greenhouses, the book also provides useful information for anyone seriously interested in plant life. The topics covered include a discussion on the advantages of having a greenhouse, types of greenhouses, learning to become familiar with tools, plans and construction techniques, actual step-by-step instructions for building several types of greenhouses, and how to supply and stock your greenhouse once it is finished. The last section of the book outlines care and maintenance of the greenhouse, handling problems that might arise, and how to make money with your greenhouse. Also included is a resources section listing names and addresses of suppliers,

INTRODUCTION

Shortly before completing the final sections of **The Plant Doctor**, my publisher asked me if I would be interested in writing a book about greenhouses. I was, of course, delighted that he had such confidence in my plant expertise and writing skills, but at the same time I was quite apprehensive about accepting such a commission. Yes, I knew something about plants, but no, I did not know much about greenhouses.

On the other hand, as a serious horticulturist, my experiences have convinced me that the more control I could have over my plants' environment, the healthier they would grow, the easier it would be to care for them, and the simpler it would be to prevent trouble or cure it if it should occur. In **The Plant Doctor**, I frequently recommend placing a plant suffering from trauma or other disorders inside a plastic bag. This bag provides a controlled environment, allowing light and intensfying humidity. It is, in fact, a sort of primitive greenhouse. But it is quite a distance from a plastic bag to a large greenhouse, and I was not at all certain that I would be up to the task of researching and writing about greenhouses.

Fortunately, my publisher had more confidence in my abilities than I did, and persuaded me to give it a try. As I began to research the book, I was pleasantly surprised to learn that cost and construction weren't nearly as prohibitive as I had feared. I also discovered that there is a wide variety of greenhouse sizes and designs. Regardless of budget, do-it-yourself experience or available space, almost anyone can build at least a basic greenhouse. My background in plants, and the assistance of friends having experience in construction, helped me to acquire a comprehensive view of how to design, build and maintain a greenhouse.

My opinion is that anyone who is serious about growing plants should have a greenhouse. That doesn't necessarily mean that you should have a large free-standing unit. Perhaps a window unit is all that you need, but you will find it of real help. Whether you spend $5 or $500, build or buy a greenhouse, select a modest window unit or an elaborate free-standing house, you will find that it will give you a certain freedom from the seasons, allow you to produce and maintain large, healthy builders and blueprints available for more elaborate greenhouses.

While the book is not intended to be encyclopedic on the subject of greenhouse construction and care, it is the most extensive book on building a greenhouse available. Whether you can afford to spend five dollars or five hundred dollars, and whether you have had construction experience or have never built anything before, you will find in this book a plan to fit your budget, your time and your degree of skill.

The Handmade Greenhouse offers a framework for learning the basic principles of building and maintaining a greenhouse, helpful to both the neophyte and the expert greenhouse gardener.

plants, and add immeasurably to your pleasure of working with green life.

Building a greenhouse can be a simple or a complicated project. It's all relative, of course, to your experience with tools and materials and the complexity of the design you choose. My advice, as one who has built a window greenhouse (with a little help from my friends), is to first try to build one of the smaller units before tackling a more ambitious design. Even if you decide to buy a pre-fabricated kit, I believe that the discussion of design principles, materials and construction techniques will make the subject clearer to you.

While this book is intended primarily for those interested in building some sort of greenhouse for themselves, I've included material on equipping and operating a greenhouse that will prove useful whether you build or buy. In addition, there is a consideration on turning your hobby into a part-time business discussed in the book's final chapter.

Researching and writing this book has been a process of discovery for me. I have found, and will discuss, the many sound, practical reasons for having a greenhouse. But I have also found another, less tangible but equally important reason for greenhouse gardening. It breeds a sense of wonder. Gardening in a greenhouse allows you to defy the seasons. You will have flowers to admire even when snow lies deeply about your house. And you will have the opportunity to become involved in, and to powerfully influence, the green life that so fascinates you.

Anyone who can use a hammer and a saw can build a greenhouse. Anyone who has at least $5 and a few extra hours on Saturday morning can build a greenhouse. And anyone who really cares about green life and backyard ecology should have a greenhouse. So if you have the ability, time, money and the inclination, **The Handmade Greenhouse** will give the help, advice and encouragement to provide a paradise for your plants.

Chapter 1

WHY A GREENHOUSE?

Plants, like people, have their wants and needs, likes and dislikes. Of course you can lavish love and affection upon your silent green friends, and they will certainly appreciate it; but plants also require **physical** affection in the form of light, heat, humidity, nutrients and oxygen as well. Give a plant all this love, and it will respond by growing larger, healthier and more rapidly.

Keep from a plant what it needs, and it will eventually die.

Often we humans, with the best of intentions, deprive our plants of one or more vital elements, such as humidity or proper nutrients. Or, equally as bad, we over-provide our plants with water or sunlight — literally killing them with kindness. Plants survival and growth are a dynamic blend of elements (as, indeed, **all** life is), and when that blend is not in proper proportion, our plants reflect that state by growing sick, inviting insect infestations, or succumbing to other maladies. After all, would you expect an exotic orchard from a Brazilian rain forest to flourish in a poorly heated, dry-aired apartment, or a shady ivy to survive in a brightly-lit window? Of course not, but sometimes the blend imbalances are so subtle that we don't recognize them until it is too late for our plants.

There is one way to be absolutely certain that all your plants receive the proper dynamic balance necessary for growth and good health, and that is by providing a controlled environment for them. By controlled environment, I mean being able to adjust the light, humidity, temperature and supply of nutriments to the **exact** proportion for your particular plant's needs. If you have central heating, you have a form of a controlled environment for people: you can adjust the heat and humidity at the turn of the dial, or counteract a hot, muggy day by switching on the air conditioner. But for plants, a controlled environment means a greenhouse.

A greenhouse, quite simply, is a structure that provides a controlled environment for plants. That includes protection from the elements, a stabilized climate and optimum growing conditions. A greenhouse is defined by its function, and not its size or shape; any enclosed structure that allows air circulation, light, humidity, water and nutrients in, in the correct proportion, can be called a greenhouse.

Why, might you ask, does a plant require so much care? Indeed, **all** life needs care and attention. Owning a cat, for example, means more than putting kitty's nightly meal out on the kitchen floor. Cats need milk or other liquids, vitamins (although many cat foods are fortified), unmatted fur, proper medical care when sick, and tender loving care. I can't say whether cats or plants are more demanding, but plants **do** have basic needs in order to grow.

Different types of plants grow best at different temperatures. By giving your plant the proper amount of heat that they need, they will do what nature intended them to do: grow. Temperatures too hot or too cold will hasten your plants' demise, however.

Light is also a necessary ingredient for plant growth because of one of nature's most basic miracles: the process of photosynthesis. Plants, unlike any other form of life, are able to manufacture their own food directly from sunlight. Give it too little light, and your plant will wither and die; give it too much light, and you may burn its leaves, or cause it to become exhausted.

Plants also need nutrients to fuel their growth because, just as man cannot live by bread alone, photosynthesis alone cannot provide a plant with all of its basic needs. A plant draws its nutrients from the soil, but just like the best-stocked pantry the soil eventually becomes empty if not refilled. The soil must be periodically replenished with plant food. Nature does this automatically outdoors through the season cycle, rain and decaying organic matter, but **you** must do it for your housebroken plants.

Plants need water in order to survive. Even the driest, dustiest cactus in the desert cannot exist without water, since water is absolutely essential for cellular growth and carrying nutriments throughout the plant.

Water by itself, however, is insufficient for your plants' good health. Most plants will not grow, not even survive, if the atmosphere is too dry. Humidity is essential to plant growth, and without it, your plant will "cannibalize" itself by drawing excessive amounts of water

through its roots to correct the imbalance, only to wilt after exausting its water supply.

Plants, like all living things, require oxygen. If you can breathe, your plant can breathe as well, but if the air is too still or stale, your plant will suffer accordingly. If your plants sit in a draft or a strong breeze, they may bend or break under the pressure, or become chilled or traumatized.

By giving your plants a balanced supply of the elements they need you encourage growth, good health and longevity. You can do this, of course, in a window sill or on a ledge. But if you are truly concerned about green life, and you want to do it much **better** in order to stimulate far greater growth than you could ever have in an uncontrolled environment, you will **need** a greenhouse. Your greenhouse is a miniature green world, and you can exercise far more control over that world than any other environment you will ever garden in.

Having your own greenhouse is neither impractical nor a luxury. A greenhouse will simplify care of your plants, reduce plant losses due to injury or illness, allow you to grow exotic species you could otherwise not easily grow, and greatly increase the ease (as well as decrease the cost) with which you can propagate numbers of plants.

Whether you have two dozen or two hundred plants, you will find that having some sort of greenhouse will be a valuable gardening tool. When I say you need a greenhouse, I **don't** necessarily mean you need a large freestanding unit. Perhaps a window greenhouse, which will fit in any window and costs as little as $25 to make, will best suit your supply of space, time, money and plants. Whatever size greenhouse you build or buy, you can be confident that you have made a wise investment.

A well managed greenhouse will save you money, and go on saving you money, year after year. It will save you money by greatly reducing the number of plants indoor gardeners lose because of inadequate or inappropriate growing conditions. Rain, wind, sudden chills or rapidly spreading infections and pests also take their toll of an outdoor gardener's collection. Greenhouses shut such weather problems out, and decrease the chance of a sudden insect or disease attack. A clean, well managed greenhouse should suffer few serious infestations or infections, while entirely eliminating the loss of plants due to weather conditions.

A greenhouse will save you money because it offers the best conditions for propagating plants, thus increasing the number and health of the plants you can grow. And the greater the number and variety of plants you can grow, the less you have to rely upon plant stores for additions to your collection.

Also, a greenhouse will increase the market value of your property. And, you might discover that you have the talent and organizational ability to regularly raise and sell crops and plants, thus turning your avocation into a lucrative part-time vocation.

In a period of economic uncertainty and constantly climbing prices, your greenhouse can be used to grow more than plants. It can be turned to the production of a year-round supply of fruits or vegetables at a fraction of the cost you would pay for produce in stores.

Because your plants are concentrated together in one area, it should take less time and running about to care for them. Because they are in a protected, controlled environment, plant losses should be greatly reduced. The ease and success with which you can propagate plants from seeds or cuttings should also save you money. I believe a greenhouse will also, in a less tangible manner, increase your sense of wonder. For in a greenhouse, as with no other kind of gardening, you have the opportunity to be very closely involved in all the processes of plant life, and to exert a real influence on them. You can take pleasure in defying the progression of the seasons by growing things all year long. And you will be involved in a positive, healthful, constantly engaging activity that will become, if it is not already, much more than "just a hobby."

So, a greenhouse is a valuable gardening tool, and if you are serious about plants you should have one, no matter how small the unit. But **when** should you build or buy it?

Whenever you can afford the time to erect and maintain it. No matter how tight your budget, there is some size unit to fit it. If you have a small plant collection, you can use a window unit to establish greater control over your plant's environment. Or you can use a small unit as a hospital for ill plants, providing a protected environment in which they can recuperate. If you have only one window with southern exposure, make the most of it by installing a window greenhouse to propagate cuttings and seeds, to grow plants, and then to remove them to other locations in your house — acting, in fact, as your own nurseryman and supplier. Thus, even the smallest of greenhouses can save you money.

If you have a house overrun with plants — plants in pots and plants in baskets, plants in tubs and plants in large planters — you certainly could use some sort of greenhouse. You can use it to cut down on the amount of time you spend running from plant to plant, watering and feeding and misting them. You can use a greenhouse to simplify your attempts at providing an acceptable climate for your plants. You can use it to make propagation easier, and thus to save yourself money.

When you find yourself devoting more and more of your spare time to plants, and when you start wondering how to increase control over the factors that affect plant growth, consider a greenhouse. But remember — only if you are serious about your gardening. A greenhouse shouldn't precede your devotion to gardening. It should be the logical outcome of your involvement.

Are there situations when even a dedicated gardener does not need a greenhouse? Certainly. No matter how dedicated you might be, if you simply don't have the time to properly care for the plants you now have, you won't have time to plan and erect a greenhouse. But do try to plan ahead to a period when you will have time to properly select and assemble a greenhouse. When it is standing and in use, you'll be amazed at how much easier it is to take care of 200 plants in one room than it was to take care of 50 plants in four rooms.

You don't need a greenhouse if you are living in a small, dark apartment. Instead, get several hardy shade-loving plants or a terrarium to help green the place.

In most situations, though, you should have sufficient time and space to build some sort of unit, no matter how small. And, if you have a long-term interest in plants, I don't think you will regret the investment of time and effort that a greenhouse initially requires. It will pay you back, with interest, in many, many ways.

Chapter 2

CONSTRUCTION

A greenhouse, strictly speaking, is not defined by its size or shape, but by what it does. Any structure that helps further green growth by creating a controlled environment is a greenhouse. A hothouse, where tropical plants are grown in their natural jungle setting, is a type of greenhouse; so is a conservatory, and so is a small, inexpensive window unit which can be built for as little as $30.

The term **greenhouse**, while admirably descriptive about the function and purpose of a controlled environmental structure, can be misleading about the possible size and shape of the unit. The best-known type of greenhouse is the large glass and aluminum structure adjoining your local flower shop or plant supplier; but there are many other structures that range from one small enough to fit on your porch to one large enough to fill up your back garden. They range from a temporary, emergency plastic bag to a modest window unit, from a freestanding geodesic dome to a lean-to add-on to your house, from a small back yard unit to a large professional-type quonset hut. They can be made of glass or plexiglass or plastic, with wood or metal frames. Greenhouses can be simple or complex, modestly priced or outrageously expensive, small or large.

Again, any structure providing a controlled environment for your plants is a greenhouse, no matter how simple or strange it looks.

A plastic bag can be converted into a temporary greenhouse. If you have a plant that has all the symptoms of trauma (see Chapter 13), or is convalescing from an infection or insect infestation, or if you have a plant suffering from a lack of humidity, place it — pot and all — inside the bag. Tie the bag shut and leave it closed for at least two days. If the plant appears recovered, remove it and return it to its accustomed place. But if the plant appears to need additional therapy, reseal the bag and keep it sealed for several more days. Some horticulturalists recommend punching small holes in the bag to provide air; others do not. It is my experience that holes are not necessary if the plant will be kept in the bag for less than a week. If the plant is to be kept in the bag for more than a week, open the bag for a half hour each day to admit fresh air.

You can also transform one of your windows into a temporary greenhouse. Choose the window that receives the greatest number of hours of sunlight, preferably morning sunlight. Tack a piece of plastic across the inner frame of the window, thus sealing the plants you have chosen for treatment between the window and the plastic. Be sure to water the plants well before you tack the plastic in place. If the window has southern exposure, use only sun-loving or exotic plants. If the window receives a bright but diffuse light, with little direct sunlight, use plants that prefer a bright indirect light source. Pin the plastic back for fifteen minute intervals twice a day to allow fresh air to circulate. Your transformed window should prove a good clinic for tired plants, or an excellent spur to growth with plants that have been lagging. However, while you may use this procedure regularly, it cannot substitute for a real greenhouse. It is of temporary therapeutic value only.

While such measures are only temporary, they point out the fact that a greenhouse can take many shapes and sizes. And these simple, but effective, experiments offer an important lesson to anyone planning a greenhouse — **use your imagination**. While you must follow certain basics in building or buying a greenhouse, by letting your imagination roam freely you can not only come up with a truly personalized greenhouse — you may also save yourself money. A greenhouse should suit your needs, and not the reverse. And remember — a greenhouse is anything that works.

If you have decided to build a greenhouse, the smallest permanent unit to consider would be a window greenhouse. Window units can be built onto the exterior or interior of a window. Very often, you can leave the original window in place, and use it to regulate the supply of air and heat in your window unit. The aluminum or wood structure is attached to the window. Sections of glass or plastic are attached to the framework and, because the frame is rectangular, they provide illumination on two short sides and a large front. You can build such a unit on a window facing in any direction, as long as the window is not badly shadowed by trees. A window unit facing south should provide enough sun to grow tropical plants. Window units facing east or west will receive enough sun to grow a variety of popular plants. And a window greenhouse attached to a north-facing window will allow you to grow plants that could not be grown just in a north window.

EXTERIOR TYPE

INTERIOR TYPE

An aluminum and glass window greenhouse can be built for about $75. A wood framed unit using glass can be built for even less, and a unit using wood and plastic can be built from scratch for as little as $30. This is the least expensive permanent greenhouse you can build. If you have a small collection of plants, a window unit should provide as much greenhouse room as you need. If your time or budget is limited, this would be the unit that could be built most rapidly. It should take no more than ten hours, spread over a weekend, to complete this unit. And if you lack the money, or the space, to build or buy an outdoor greenhouse, you can still enjoy the pleasures and rewards of greenhouse gardening by constructing a window unit.

Plans for a simple window greenhouse are given in this book. Only a few hand tools are required, and no special skills at carpentry or construction are needed. I recommend it as an excellent first project for those with limited building experience.

Most other types of greenhouses are designed to be erected outdoors. You can purchase plans for a variety of greenhouse designs and build the unit you want yourself, or you can buy a pre-fabricated kit from a greenhouse manufacturer.

There are two basic kinds of greenhouses: freestanding and lean-to. Lean-to greenhouses are so named because they are always attached to, and leaning against, the wall of another building. Freestanding units are structurally self-supporting and unattached to other buildings.

Lean-to units have two short walls, one long side wall facing outwards, a door in one of the end walls, and a roof. Lean-to units resemble even-span freestanding units in their basic structure. An even-span house is freestanding and has a roof of equal dimensions on either side. Indeed, a lean-to rather resembles an even-span unit that has been cut in half along its ridge line, while half of the structure had been propped against a wall for support.

Although all lean-to units share a basic design idea, freestanding greenhouses come in a variety of shapes, including domes, A-frames, quonsets and even-spans.

Lean-to units are among the most inexpensive outdoor greenhouses you can build or buy. Only freestanding units using light weight frames and plastic are less expensive. You use less material in building a lean-to greenhouse, and that is where the greatest cost savings come from In addition, it is often significantly less expensive to heat, light and supply water, as the unit can be connected directly to your home utilities without running special lines or pipes far outside the house. By

positioning your lean-to over one of your windows, you can further decrease heating costs by simply opening the window on cold days. While you cannot entirely heat your greenhouse in this manner, you can decrease the size, and thus the cost, of the heater you will have to buy for the unit.

LEAN-TO

If you have a small yard, a lean-to will offer the most economical use of space. But remember that you must have a rain gutter running along the roof above your unit to carry away the rain run-off that might otherwise damage the greenhouse roof.

A lean-to can be built only on the southern or eastern walls of your home. Because it has just half the light-transmitting surface of a freestanding unit, it needs all the light it can get.

Building a lean-to will require the use of more tools and construction skills than constructing a window greenhouse. In addition, you will have to lay some sort of foundation or build an elevated floor (see Chapter 8). Lean-tos are more expensive than window units, and you cannot build a lean-to unit for less than several hundred dollars. You should have some experience with basic construction before you attempt to build such a unit. If you decide not to build at this time, a number of greenhouse manufacturers offer pre-fab lean-to kits. But remember, even if you buy a kit, you will still have to lay the foundation or install an elevated floor yourself, or pay someone to do it.

Outdoor greenhouses should be at least 6½′ high at the ridge line, the center and highest portion of the roof. Either lean-to or freestanding units should have a width of at least 5′, and they may have a length of from 6′ to 20′, depending on the time, money and skill you bring to the job.

A freestanding even-span greenhouse is among the most expensive designs you can build or buy, especially when the materials used in construction include a framework of aluminum and panes or sheets of glass.

FREESTANDING EVEN SPAN

Even-span units have a shape (as viewed from the front) rather like that of a tent. There is a high center ridge, a roof of even length sloping downwards from either side of the ridge of the roof, and a more modest slope, or a straight wall, running downwards from the point where the roof meets the sides of the house. There are two long side walls, and two short end walls. One of the end walls has a door. The house can be made entirely of glass or plastic, not including the frame, or it might also have a low brick or concrete wall extending about 2′ above the ground.

Plans for most even-span units call for a height of from 7′ to 8′, and a length of at least 8′. While I have been quoting exact measurements in order to give you an idea of size ranges, most plans and pre-fab kits call for heights and lengths of feet **and** inches. Although it is no more difficult to work in feet and inches, it can be rather confusing trying to read and remember them.

Freestanding even-span units are large and attractive, and can be erected in a variety of locations. Because they have such a large light-transmitting surface, they can even be established in areas too overcast for other types of units, such as a lean-to. However, they not only cost more to build but more to run. You must extend the utilities — electricity and water — out to them. And because they are open on all sides to the elements, they cost more to heat. There is no question, though, that even-span units are one of — if not the most — popular of designs.

You can build and furnish a basic even-span unit for as little as $350-$400. Even-spans requiring more elaborate and expensive kinds of materials will obviously cost more. Don't expect to build and furnish an even-span greenhouse using an aluminum or wood frame for less than $650. It is not uncommon for people to spend well over a thousand dollars for building and furnishing a large even-span unit.

Greenhouse manufacturers produce a number of pre-fab even-span kits, in a price range of from $225 to $900. Remember that the cost of a pre-fab does not include the cost of either laying a foundation or building an elevated floor. With that in mind, it seems to me that you can build a modest even-span greenhouse for about the same amount you can buy one. However, even-span houses require a familiarity with tools and some skill and experience in construction. If you have never built anything sizable before, I do not recommend that you begin your education by attempting to build an even-span from the ground up.

A Dutch light (or glass-to-ground) house has an even-span design. The only difference is that the Dutch light has no low wall, but instead has glass or plastic running down to just above ground level, where there may be a single row of bricks. Dutch light units do very well in a sunny location, but they can also be used on more shadowed ground, as they are almost totally light-transmitting structures.

An 8' long by 5' wide Dutch light unit made of a wooden frame and plastic should cost about $450 to build. The use of aluminum and glass to build such a unit would drive the cost up to at least $600, and possibly as high as $800.

A simple Dutch light unit may be somewhat less complicated to construct than a typical even-span unit, but it will still require some experience and skill with a variety of tools (see Chapter 6 for a description of the tools needed to build a greenhouse or assemble a kit). I don't recommend that you attempt such a project unless you have had some previous construction experience or can rely on the close help of someone who has. There are several pre-fabricated Dutch light kits available. The Agricultural Extension Service publishes a plan for a homemade version of the Dutch light, using wood and plastic.

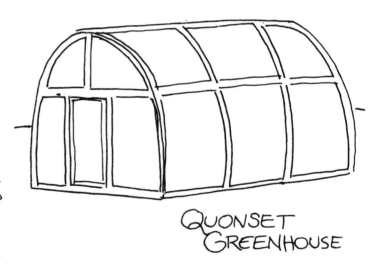

QUONSET GREENHOUSE

DUTCH LIGHT TYPE

Quonset greenhouses, so named because of their similarity in shape to the familiar all-purpose armed services pre-fab, are sturdy structures, relatively easy to assemble and less expensive than even-span units.

Quonsets need a sunny location. And, as with all freestanding units, you will have to run utility lines to them. While you may be able to build a quonset frame of wood and plastic (10' long, 6' wide) for as little as $250-$300, this estimate does not include the cost of a foundation.

Quonsets are not difficult to construct, if, again, you have some expertise with tools. You need not belong to the carpenters local, but you must have previously attempted some projects built with wood before you can safely approach building **any** sort of freestanding greenhouse.

Some manufacturers offer pre-fab quonset kits. Published plans for building your own quonset, and for building other large freestanding units are listed in the bibliography.

hold the majority of plants in a greenhouse, are designed with a long, even-sided structure in mind. To make the most of space in a dome greenhouse, you will have to build your own curved benches or work out some other alternative.

There is a plan for a simple dome unit given in Chapter 9. Other plans for dome structures are listed in the bibliography. Several pre-fab dome greenhouse kits are now on the market, and are listed in the appendix. While costs for a homemade or pre-fab dome may vary widely, depending on the size of the unit and the materials used in construction (once again, aluminum and glass are the most expensive materials, wood and plastic being less expensive), a dome will cost no less than $150 to build, and can cost considerably more.

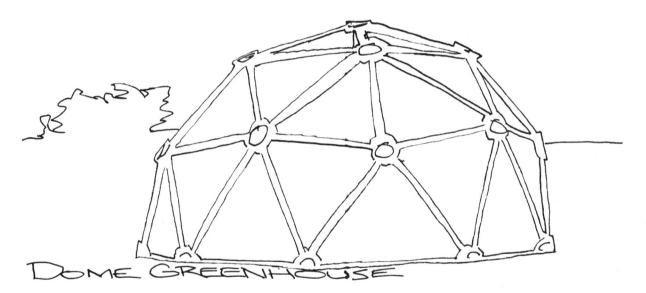

DOME GREENHOUSE

Domes are the most recent additions to greenhouse styles. Their most impressive feature is that, like the glass-to-ground greenhouse, almost all of their surface area is light-transmitting. In addition, their unique circular shapes make them unusual and appealing to many people. However, their shape may also be a drawback. Benches, the "tables with sides" which

These are the basic greenhouse designs. While there are many other styles, all of them derive from one or another of these basics. Choose the design you want with deliberation, taking into account such information as the amount of space and sunlight available, the time you can afford to build and care for a unit, and the amount of money you can invest in the project.

COLDFRAMES AND HOTBEDS

Coldframes and hotbeds are, in effect, miniature greenhouses. They have four wooden sides, are bottomless, sunk partially in the ground, and have a light-admitting surface of either glass or plastic.

Two inch redwood is frequently recommended in the construction of coldframes. Because glass sashes are available from suppliers in 3x6' sizes, coldframes are generally at least this large, and may be increased in size in multiples of that measurement, to accomodate more sashes. If you are using plastic to cover the unit, or are employing a window frame salvaged from a demolished house, you can alter the measurements to fit your purposes.

Four 4x4'' posts should be driven 3'' into the ground. Within that area, remove the ground soil to a depth of one half to one full foot. Place the frame in the ground, and fill in the bottom with a layer of gravel, and then a layer of sand (some gardeners place a layer of straw between the gravel and sand). Then pour in a layer of soil, of from 6'' to 10'' in depth. Tamp the soil down, and moisten it with a spray of water — **don't** pour in a lot of water.

Some gardeners hinge the top, or sash, to provide easier access. That is up to you — but you must have a thermometer on one of the inner walls of the unit. Regularly check the thermometer, and if the temperature has climbed higher than your gardening calls for, prop open the sash or partially remove the plastic to permit cooling circulation.

Your coldframe should be located on a well-drained plot of land, facing south so as to receive as much sunlight as possible. White or silver paint on the unit's inner walls will further increase the amount and intensity of light available.

When the weather turns cool, you can insulate the unit by building banks of soil along its sides. During cold nights, and on cold, sunless winter days cover the top of the unit with straw, wood planks laid over burlap or whatever other materials you think might add protection.

During very sunny summer days, you may have to provide some shading for the unit, by draping a sheet of translucent plastic over the sash or by stretching cheese cloth on a frame over the unit. If you have used glass for the top of the coldframe, you can paint the panes with one of the shading compounds available for use on greenhouses.

Although you cannot stand in a coldframe to work, and it cannot serve to exhibit choice plants, as a greenhouse can, it can be a useful adjunct to greenhouse gardening. You can use your coldframe as a propagating unit to raise plants from seed, to prepare summer vegetables and flowers as much as two month ahead of time, to "force" bulbs into early flowering, and to grow new plants from cuttings.

A hotbed is a coldframe with heating equipment added. Probably the simplest method for turning a coldframe into a hotbed is to purchase soil heating cables. Unless you are familiar with wiring, it would be a good idea to have an electrician install the cables. The cables, which are powered by electric current, should be buried in the floor of the unit under a 1 to 2 inch layer of topsoil or an inch of sand. If you wish to use a coldframe year round, you will have to supply some source of warmth. In previous times, gardeners made do with layers of manure.

If you are unable to construct a greenhouse a coldframe or hotbed can fulfill many of its functions, and can be constructed quite inexpensively. Or, if you have a greenhouse you may find having a coldframe quite useful. It can be used exclusively for propagating plants from seeds or cuttings, or for growing several types of plants requiring the same conditions, thus freeing space within the greenhouse for more plants.

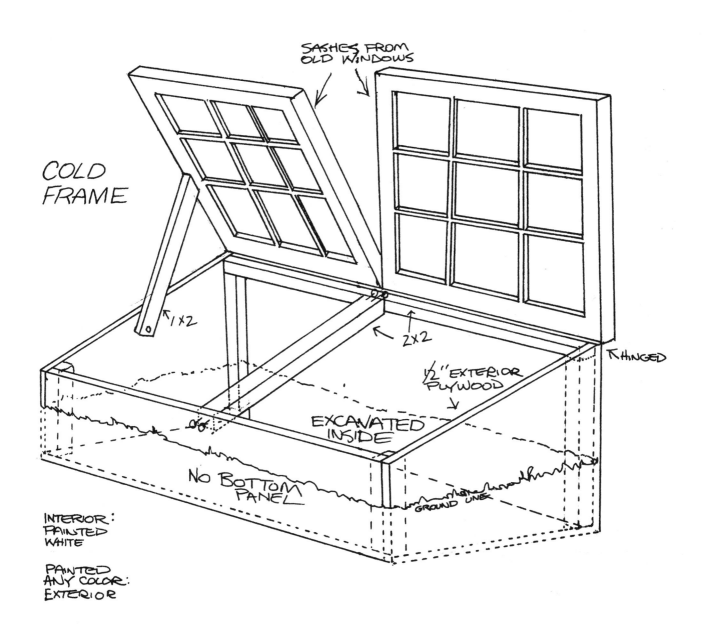

SASHES FROM OLD WINDOWS

COLD FRAME

1 X 2

2 X 2

½" EXTERIOR PLYWOOD

HINGED

EXCAVATED INSIDE

NO BOTTOM PANEL

GROUND LINE

INTERIOR: PAINTED WHITE

PAINTED ANY COLOR: EXTERIOR

Chapter 3

BUILD OR BUY?

"Buy it, don't build it" is the advice offered in many greenhouse books. And, at first, it does seem as if buying a prefabricated kit is the most sensible course to take. After all, doesn't it always cost less to buy a greenhouse kit than to design and build your own unit? And doesn't it require far less time, effort and skill to assemble a kit than to build your own unit?

My answer to both questions would have to be both yes and no. For the matter of buying versus building is just not that simple.

Let's first consider the cost factor.

Several dozen companies design and market greenhouses in pre-fabricated kits. These kits are available in a wide range of sizes and prices. They are also sold in a variety of styles, including even-span, lean-to, Dutch light, quonset and dome-type units. The kits are usually shipped directly from the manufacturer packed flat in large boxes.

The kits include pre-measured and pre-cut pieces of wood or metal for the frame, glass, plastic or fiberglass to provide illumination, and all of the nails, nuts, screws, bolts or putty necessary to firmly hold the materials together. Many kits are advertised as being capable of assembly with the use of a few easy-to-use hand tools. All you need do is follow the detailed instructions included in the kit, they say. The prices for these kits begin at about $150, and some go as high as $1,000.

But the price that you see in a catalog does **not** include the cost of such necessary equipment as a heater, it does **not** include the price of plant benches, and it does **not** include the cost of the foundation or floor you must prepare for the unit. What you get for the price printed beneath that attractive photo is the house, and nothing **but** the house. Many kit brochures neglect to tell you that the unit cannot securely stand without some sort of floor or foundation to anchor it. You also must have a heater for use during the early spring, fall and winter. And you really cannot properly use a greenhouse until you have benches upon which to stand your plants. All but the smallest of greenhouses should also have some sort of humidifying system.

So don't decide on a kit, as opposed to building your own unit, until you have calculated **all** the costs of assembling a greenhouse. And remember, a unit is of little use unless you have the equipment necessary to run it.

Price a number of kits. Price the accessories. Then, compare it to the cost of buying your own materials and accessories according to the list supplied with the plans for building your own greenhouse. A foundation (or flooring) will cost the same whether you buy or build a unit. Once you compare the true price tags for comparable homemade and pre-fab units, I believe that you will find in many cases there is very little difference between buying a pre-fab or building a unit from scratch.

The confusion that can arise over the "hidden" costs of buying a greenhouse is illustrated in the following letter given to me in the course of my research.

"A friend of mine," the author of the letter writes, "was told by phone by a salesman (sic) from one of the most prestigious manufacturers that the greenhouse he wanted was just $1,000. On this understanding, he agreed to an appointment to specify in detail and order his greenhouse. The salesman arrived and began writing down what was needed — the upshot was that by the time my friend had [a price quotation for] a complete greenhouse, he had a $4,000 tab for the thing (which at that time represented the greenhouse he thought he'd get for $1,000.) He didn't buy it."

You can't get a functioning greenhouse for the prices quoted in a catalog. You get the house, and then you must lay a foundation or build a floor, and you must get several pieces of essential equipment. Some manufacturers now offer units that come with stakes that can be driven into the ground and serve as an anchor for the unit in place of an expensive concrete foundation. But unless the catalog specifies such a feature, you must assume that you will have to provide some sort of foundation or flooring yourself (see Chapter 8).

Most suppliers' catalogs also include a section on equipment, which should allow you to price and compare necessary furnishings.

If you find a pre-fab kit that seems tailored to your needs and budget (with the other costs added in, remember), consider the company that makes it. Keep in mind this incident, also related in the letter quoted above.

"A man once spent an hour or so describing the merits of a line of devastatingly low cost greenhouses of glass to me — a line he knew only from pictures. I knew there had to be a fly in the ointment somewhere, but having no experience of the unit, kept quiet. A few days later, I chanced to mention the unit to another nurseryman, and his response was 'Yeah, I ordered one of those once. It took three of my men a week to build it!' It seems that it was rather hastily made, pieces didn't fit, and to cap it all off, it was missing considerable hardware."

Now it's unlikely that such trouble will befall you, but you shouldn't buy your unit through the mails without first contacting the manufacturer. If the company has an area representative within traveling distance of your home, they will probably get in touch with you. Then if you are seriously interested in their unit, make an appointment with the salesman. Find out as much as you can about the greenhouse you want from him. Ask him to help you calculate the total cost of a functioning greenhouse. And ask him if he could put you in touch with people in your area who own the unit. If there is no sales representative in your area, write directly to the company with your questions, and a request for a list of names of those people in your area who have purchased the same unit. Try calling some of the owners up and ask them what they think of their units. How difficult were they to assemble? Did they run into any trouble with the units? Are they sturdy and do they work well? I have found greenhouse owners to be among the most helpful of people, especially when they hear you are considering getting your own greenhouse.

Most greenhouse manufacturers offer some form of a guarantee with their kits. Read it carefully before you buy. After your unit is shipped and you find that something is missing or defective, get in touch immediately with the supplier. Your guarantee should cover the replacement without cost of defective or missing parts.

Can a pre-fab kit be assembled more rapidly and more easily than a unit from raw materials? Of course it can. And if you have a very limited amount of free time, but you want a greenhouse, your best bet is a pre-fab. But keep in mind when estimating the time it will take to erect a pre-fab that at least one day will have to be set aside to lay a foundation or build flooring. And the foundation will have to stand for several days before you can begin assembling the unit on top of it.

Many medium-sized outdoor greenhouses can be assembled from a kit in two long days, provided you have at least one other pair of helping hands. The larger and more complex the greenhouse, the more time it will require to assemble.

It is possible to build some simple outdoor greenhouses over a weekend, if you have done all of the preparatory work, such as marking out the dimensions of the greenhouse and assembling all the necessary materials and parts. Most handmade outdoor units require at least several weekends to build. Some, however, will take even longer.

Some greenhouse manufacturers state that certain of their models can be assembled with the use of several simple hand tools.

Certainly all pre-fab kits are designed with simplicity of assembly in mind. Because so much of the planning, measuring and cutting is done in the factory, no special skill is required to put a unit together. However, many of the kits are more difficult to assemble than the brochures would have you believe.

The same cannot be said of building your own unit. You should not attempt to build an outdoor greenhouse from most plans unless you have had some experience working with wood (or metals, depending on what material your frame will be made of) and with a variety of tools, or unless you can rely on the advice and assistance of someone experienced in such matters.

There are several excellent reasons for building, rather than buying your greenhouse. There is the possibility that you will be able to save money. You can adapt your unit to your own specific needs, and not the other way around (as is often the case with pre-fabs). And you can take pleasure and satisfaction from having tackled a demanding job and succeeded.

In summary, don't decide to build a greenhouse simply because it **might** save you money. It might, and then it might not. Build it because you want to do it yourself, and because you know how. Build it because you want it to be **your** greenhouse, from first to last.

If you don't have the knowledge to build from the start a large outdoor greenhouse, don't assume that you then must buy a pre-fab. There are several units that can be built from the raw materials relatively quickly, and with a minimum of construction skills.

"Build it, or buy it?" Buy it if you are pressed for time, and want to get your greenhouse in operation as soon as possible. Buy it if you want a large unit, and you have little previous experience with construction techniques or tools.

Build it, if you have the time and the determination to do it just the way you want. Build it, if you have priced the unit you want and found that you can build it for less than you can buy it. Build it because you want to build it. If you lack the skills to build a complex unit, settle for one of the simpler homemade designs.

Chapter 4
SITE SELECTION

You should erect your greenhouse where it will receive the most hours of sunlight each day. A greenhouse is designed to make the most of natural light, while enclosing plants in a protected, artificially controlled environment. While you can always shade your plants from light that is too intense (as it can be on some summer days — see Chapter 10), you will find it much more difficult — and quite costly — to supplement the sunlight in a perpetually dim location.

The best location for your greenhouse would be in a window or on a plot of land having a southern exposure. However, if that isn't possible, an east or west-facing site should receive sufficient light to grow many plant species. And if you can build your greenhouse only in a window or on a plot of ground having northern exposure, by all means do so. There are many hardy plants that prefer a shady location. There are bound to be some areas within the unit that will receive sufficient sunlight to grow sun-loving plants. Or, at an additional expense, you can install an artificial light system to supplement the natural light you receive. With such a system, you should be able to grow even tropical sun-loving plants. However, you should not build a lean-to on the north side of your house. Because it has less light-transmitting surface, it cannot give plants even the indirect light that they would require.

Use a compass to determine locations around your house and property. Check out likely sites and windows by calculating how many hours of sunlight each location receives. The location averaging the greatest number of hours of bright light, and meeting the other requirements discussed below, is the spot you want. If you are investigating potential sites during the winter, the rule-of-thumb is that any location receiving at least four hours of winter sunlight is acceptable.

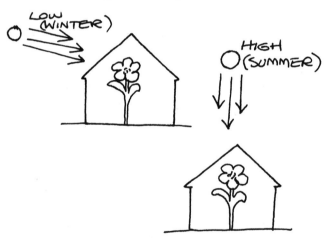

Finding a choice spot is not always so simple a matter. Perhaps the location receiving the most hours of sunlight is too small for the type of house you had in mind. Perhaps trees obscure the window or the site that you like best. And perhaps the condition of the land presents serious difficulties of construction. If so, go on to the next most likely spot. Unless you are in the depths of a forest or a high-rise jungle there should be at least one window, or one small plot of ground, that has sufficient light falling upon it to illuminate a greenhouse.

Erect your unit on a relatively flat site; otherwise it will prove to be hard work to fill in uneven land or remove major obstacles. Don't commit yourself to the labor of uprooting tree stumps and digging out thick skeins of roots unless you have no alternative. Wherever you build outdoors, make certain that you aren't building over utility pipes or wires. If they should have to be excavated at some later date, what will happen to your greenhouse?

What if the only available outdoor site is on a hillside? If that is all you have, use it. But build on the **south** side of the hill, to give your plants the sunshine they will need. Don't build your greenhouse at the bottom of a hill: cold air, being heavier than warm air, collects in depressions in the landscape, and will send your heating bill rocketing upwards. Don't build on a slope having a serious problem with water runoff. And please don't attempt to build on unstable land — remember that biblical proverb about a man building his house on sand? Marshy ground, or ground that drains badly after a rainstorm, or land that is frequently flooded, are all undesirable locations for greenhouses.

If your property has few trees, and if strong winds sweep across it during the winter, try to build your unit away from the prevailing path of the wind. A strong wind blowing across your greenhouse in winter can drive up heating costs and might, if the wind

carries debris, rip holes in plastic or shatter glass panes. Even in the summer a pronounced wind can be dangerous, as a dry wind will suck moisture out of the air, or be chill enough to traumatize plants.

If wind does present a problem, you can do several things to lessen the impact of the air currents. You can build a lean-to unit. Because it is so close to the house, it is much less exposed to the full force of winds. You can blunt the effect of the wind on a large freestanding greenhouse by planting a hedge or building a fence in the path of the prevailing wind. But build such a wind screen at least 10' from the greenhouse, to make certain that no shadow will fall across the plants.

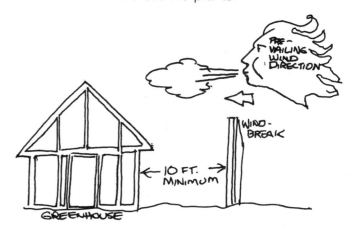

You **know** that you should not build a greenhouse beneath trees — unless you want an expensive tool shed or summer house. But what about those trees that seem such a safe distance away from your site? Check each potential location several times one day, to determine whether the trees cast shadows across your site at some point. Deciduous trees (those that shed their leaves with a change of season) may pose no problem if they are not grouped thickly together, casting dense shadows over long hours of the day. Indeed, they may be of some help, for in summer their shadows may somewhat dilute the intensity of the brilliant sun. Large evergreens can mean trouble, for they do not become bare in the fall, and they will continue to cast a shadow during those dim winter days when your plants will need as much light as they can get.

If you think that an otherwise acceptable location is overshadowed by large trees, it would probably be wisest to look for another location. It is too costly and time consuming to remove large old trees. It is also destructive. Trees are too valuable a part of green life on this planet to sacrifice them for the sake of a greenhouse.

There is another factor to be considered in your selection of a site for an outdoor greenhouse: cost. The further away from your house you erect a unit, the further you will have to run utility lines (electricity and water). When you calculate the cost of a large freestanding greenhouse, keep this factor of distance in mind. For while there are methods for reducing the costs of utilities in running a greenhouse, there is no way to get along entirely without them. (See Chapter 10)

In summer, sunlight is the determining factor in selecting a location for your greenhouse. But you must also take into consideration the nature of the land that you intend to build upon, whether it requires extensive clearing or filling in, whether it has good drainage, and whether it is badly overshadowed by large trees.

Don't take on unnecessary labors in building a greenhouse on a sunny site. If the land offers too many difficulties, go on to the next sunniest site. And if the best location you can manage receives only indirect light, remember that you can, at some additional continuing expense, install electric lighting to supplement the supply of natural light.

Choosing a location for your greenhouse is not something that can be lightly done. But neither is it something technically difficult or time-consuming. The most important thing you need to select a good site is your common sense.

26

Chapter 5

READING PLANS

After you have selected the type of greenhouse that you feel best meets your needs and budget, and after you have chosen a suitable location for the unit, you then must select a plan. This plan, based on the style of greenhouse you have decided to erect, should include a detailed estimate of the sizes, shapes and quantities of all the materials you will need. You should also have a list, with sketches, of the order and methods to be followed in putting the materials together to make your greenhouse.

Manufacturers of pre-fabricated greenhouse kits supply step-by-step instructions with their products, explaining what you must do and in what order you must do it. Most of the difficult work of measuring and cutting pieces has already been done. If, however, you intend to build a unit starting from scratch, you may secure detailed plans for building a greenhouse from several sources. Your county agricultural officer, listed in the phone directory under U.S. GOVERNMENT, should be able to refer you to free, readily available plans published by the government. Or you can select one of the units for which plans are given in this book. There are, in addition, several books presently on the market that offer plans for building greenhouses. These are listed in the bibliography at the end of this book.

Unless you have had experience drafting plans or blueprints, I suggest that you choose a plan from one of the sources cited above. Drawing up your own plans can prove to be a frustrating experience if you don't have a grasp of proportion, scale and other techniques of technical drafting. There are enough plans available for you to find at least one that will meet your particular needs.

Collect as many plans as you can, and carefully study each of them. The plan you use should have an exact list of all necessary materials, a detailed explanation of procedures, several diagrams to indicate clearly the steps you should take and the patterns of the material you should use. A good plan should have a clear, readable style that does not confuse you or obscure any of the procedures. And it should be thorough. If you find a plan that fulfills many of your needs, but is not specific enough, consult your agricultural agent or ask a friend with experience in construction for details.

How do you "read" a plan? Begin by reading the title. It will specify the subject of the plan. A plan for a lean-to greenhouse will say so, and the title may also indicate some of the materials to be used. ("A Plan for an Inexpensive Plastic Lean-to Greenhouse"). Next, read all of the instructions printed on the margins of the plan. Then take a look at the diagrams included with the instructions. These diagrams are generally keyed, by a number or letter, to specific points in the text, and to illustrate features of the unit or procedures in its construction.

The diagrams should present different views of the structure, as seen from different perspectives, usually including views from above, from the front, sides and back. The diagrams are composed of several kinds of lines. These lines include:

Working lines, which represent the edges of surfaces. Working lines are always the heaviest, darkest lines in a diagram. They describe, in effect, either the shape of the structure or some part of the structure being built, or one of the materials being used in the structure.

Dotted lines are used to indicate working lines that would obscure the other features of a particular view.

Dimension lines indicate the size of some part of the structure. They are the lines drawn between two working lines to show the distance between those working lines. The numbers printed along or next to the dimension lines state the measurement of that distance.

Extension lines extend outward from some working lines, to that point where the dimension line may be drawn in to indicate a measurement. They are used when there is not sufficient room within the working lines to indicate measurements without confusing the drawing.

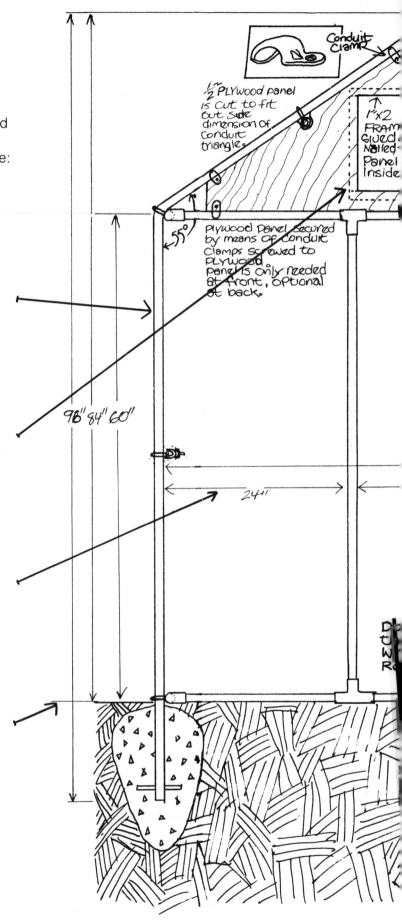

Some construction data and measurements may be included in the margins of the diagrams, as opposed or in addition to being included in the paragraphs describing the project and explaining procedures. Some plans even include a legend to explain construction terms.

Also included in the margin of the plan (usually on the right-hand side) is the scale of the diagrams. Most plans are drawn to scale, to indicate an exact relation between the size of a line and the size of an actual part of the structure. The length of the working lines are the same length in relation to one another as the proportions of the structure itself. For instance, a scale of $\frac{1}{3}'' = 1'$ would mean that $\frac{1}{3}''$ in the diagram is equivalent to $1'$ of the actual structure. Not all plans are drawn to scale, however. If they are not, they should be so marked.

After you have read and re-read the directions and matched them to the diagrams, try sketching the plan out to be certain that you understand it. If you are puzzled about anything, go back and study it again. Ask questions. Or consult one of several books available on basic terms and procedures of construction (see bibliography).

If the instructions included with your pre-fabricated kit seem unclear and no amount of study will resolve the problem, write to the manufacturer requesting an explanation.

When you plan a greenhouse, make it a rule to ask questions. Of the firms producing greenhouses. Of friends with construction experience. Of your county agricultural agent. And of acquaintances who have bought and assembled or built their own units. Any local horticulture society might also provide some useful, knowledgeable contacts.

If you select a clear, detailed plan, and if you study it until you are sure you understand it, you should be able to simplify building your own unit. The point is to do all of your preliminary work **thoroughly** — don't let yourself in for any unnecessary setbacks, hidden costs or surprises.

A good plan, and your mastery of it, is the first step in building a sturdy, well functioning greenhouse.

Chapter 6
MATERIALS

Today, the plant grower shopping for a greenhouse pre-fab kit or for the materials to build his own unit is often confronted by a bewildering variety of materials. It wasn't always so.

Not too many years ago greenhouses were restricted to the estates of the wealthy and the back lots of agricultural colleges. Greenhouses were imposingly large structures, fashioned of wood, metal and glass. Greenhouse manufacturers were those few men who designed and built the costly buildings, one at a time.

It took several parallel developments to turn a luxury into a mass market commodity. Light-weight metal alloys and the development of the assembly line combined to make possible the construction of light-weight and relatively inexpensive greenhouses. Alloys made the framework of a greenhouse so light that it could be shipped without prohibitive cost throughout the country. Assembly line production made it possible to significantly reduce the price, and dramatically increase the availability of a variety of greenhouses. The remarkable upturn of interest in all types of home gardening during and after World War II created a new market for the mass produced greenhouse. Finally, the introduction of fiberglass and several forms of heavy plastic as substitutes for glass brought the price of a simple greenhouse down even

further, and the continuing growth of interest in gardening insured a market for the ever lighter, ever less expensive greenhouse.

What are the basic materials out of which a greenhouse is made? They include wood, aluminum, glass, fiberglass and plastic.

Only two kinds of wood can be used for the framework of a greenhouse: redwood and cypress.

Only these two woods are resistant enough to moisture to withstand the high humidity of a greenhouse without rotting. Cypress is used less often in greenhouse construction because it is harder to buy, and not because it is in any way inferior.

A number of greenhouse manufacturers make their frames of redwood. It is light, durable, shrinks very little and is remarkably resistant, like cypress, to insects, moisture and decay. It is said to be an easy wood to work with.

If you are buying wood to build your own greenhouse, buy only **heart** cypress or **heart** redwood. The term refers to that part of the tree the wood has been cut from. Sapwood is the new growth of a tree, forming its outer layers. Heartwood is the inner portion of a tree, and is the older growth.

Aluminum is now used for the frames of many greenhouse kits. It is light but sturdy, does not rot or warp and will not require a sealant such as paint (as wooden framework does). But it is somewhat more expensive and can be difficult to cut if you are unfamiliar with the material. Not all types of aluminum can be cut or shaped with hand tools. If you are pricing aluminum for a homemade greenhouse, be sure to tell the salesman what you want it for. And if you do decide to work with it, remember that it throws off a "hard" sawdust when it is worked on power tools, so wear safety goggles.

Glass has always been a distinguishing feature of greenhouses. But increasingly, both manufacturers and backyard builders are turning to more pliable and less expensive materials, such as plexiglass and plastic.

Certainly both plexiglass and plastic are easier to work than glass. They are also less expensive and will not shatter. Plexiglass is generally very tough, and quite resistant to blows. Plastic, however, can be torn. Both are lighter than glass — meaning that the framework need not be so heavy to support them, and therefore a lighter, less expensive framework can be used. A lighter greenhouse is also easier to erect.

I have been told that both plexiglass and several types of plastic transmit **more** light than glass.

While plexiglass will last, some types of plastic must be replaced every year. In addition, snow can prove a disaster for a plastic greenhouse if not continuously removed.

The movement among greenhouse manufacturers seems to be towards more and more lightweight but durable materials. In addition, several large firms (like Monsanto) keep adding newer and newer plastic-like materials to the market.

Glass and aluminum are among the most expensive materials used to build greenhouses. Wood is somewhat less expensive than aluminum. Plexiglass and the many types of durable plastic now available are generally less expensive than glass.

If you intend to build a unit, I suggest that you carefully investigate the variety of materials on the market. Some of them, notably the plastics, can greatly reduce the cost of construction. Shop around. Several large chemical concerns will provide you with information of the synthetics they make, and how they may be used in construction. Check the bibliography for sources of information on materials.

If you are buying a greenhouse kit, the hard work of measuring, cutting and shaping materials will have been done for you. But you should still know something about the qualities of each material and what it adds to the cost of a unit.

You may choose the materials for your house in one of two ways. Many published greenhouse plans describe exactly what materials should be used, how they should be used, and in what quantity they are needed. Or, if you are substituting materials or working on your own plans, the most important factors to consider in selecting materials are comparative costs, durability, the ease with which a material can be used and its resistance to environmental damage (snow, hail, rain). Choose your materials on the basis of what you have to spend and how easy or difficult they are to work with. Also, consider the ease or difficulty of maintenance. While aluminum may be slightly more costly to buy, it requires less upkeep than wood over the years. Whatever plans or materials you finally decide upon, make certain that they best meet your budget needs, time availability and skill requirements.

USED MATERIALS

"Recycled" materials, a friend calls them, and I admit to liking the term, and the concept he's referring to. In many locations, time and persistence will be all you need to find a variety of inexpensive "used" building materials — materials that will help you decrease the cost of your greenhouse. Although I have never been aware of it until my friend pointed it out to me, there are several companies in my area, including a demolition firm, having large inventories of doors and window framers, plumbing fixtures and other materials, all removed from buildings that have been demolished. While the condition of these supplies will vary widely, you may well be able to find some items in good enough shape to be used in your greenhouse. And you will need to spend only a fraction of what such items would cost you when they were new.

Check your Yellow Pages for a listing of demolition companies in your area. Many "wreckers" maintain warehouses filled with salvaged materials. Or, you might know of other small firms in your area that sell salvaged materials. Of particular interest for the greenhouse would be a "recycled" door. Unless the wood is chipped, warped or otherwise damaged, there is no reason why a "used" door will not give just as good service as a "new" door. I have seen doors in excellent condition priced as low as $4 in one warehouse, and I do not believe such a price to be an exception.

However, don't plan on such a buy before you find it — that is, there is no way you can be sure of finding a door of just the dimensions your plans require. Shop for a door first, and if you find a good one, alter the dimensions of the plan to accomodate it.

It may be that you can salvage the glass from used window frames for "recycling" on the roof of your unit. Window frames, **with** the glass intact, cost as little as $3 per window at some warehouses. That's considerably less than the price of the glass involved, if it were purchased new. And while I don't recommend it, some people do make their greenhouses from a series of window frames bolted together. I think it is a very difficult to control the environment in such a unit, as they seem to tend to being either overheated or very drafty. However, it's your greenhouse, and if you choose to do it that way by all means go to a wrecker for your supply of frames.

Your search might also uncover a sink of just the right size for your unit. Many such sinks still have the faucets attached, and all you need do is replace the washers in the faucets and thoroughly scrub the sink out. Sinks cost anywhere from $10 to $15, making them a real bargain. Again — look for a sink first, and **then** adapt your plans to fit it in.

Some wreckers stock the bricks removed

from demolished buildings. The bricks, costing perhaps a dime apiece, can be used to make your foundation, a walkway within the unit or to build the low solid wall built from the ground up, on all but glass-to-ground greenhouses.

Some secondhand dealers also carry a variety of heating units. If you consider buying one to adapt for your greenhouse, inspect it carefully. Has it been rebuilt? What sort of condition does it appear to be in? Is there any sort of guarantee to cover it? While I believe that buying your heating unit new is a worthwhile investment, if your funds are limited or your spirit adventurous, you might want to give a secondhand unit a try. It's up to you.

If you can find a supplier of such items in your area, I suggest you seriously consider incorporating them in your greenhouse. If they are in good shape, some soap and water and a coat of paint will have them looking as good as new. And the idea of recycling is a pleasing one — you're saving something that would otherwise go to waste, and you're saving yourself some money that can be applied to other important items in your greenhouse.

Chapter 7
TOOLS

The tools you need to build a greenhouse are neither difficult to obtain nor to use. They are the basic hand tools used in the construction and maintenance of most wooden or metal structures. If you regularly do repairs around your house or apartment, you probably own some of the tools you will require already. Any additional tools you might need can be readily purchased at a hardware or department store.

Several pre-fabricated greenhouse kits now on the market are advertised as requiring only the simplest of hand tools for assembly. The majority of the plans for building your own greenhouse given in this book, as well as some of the other available do-it-yourself greenhouse plans, require only a small number of easy-to-use tools, including a hammer, hand saw, hand or electric drill and a screwdriver.

Many pre-fabricated kits, and all elaborate designs for large homemade greenhouses, require the use of a wider variety of hand tools, however.

Whether you buy or build a unit, you will be using tools to assemble it. And for even the simplest of units, you will be using several different types of tools — each type for a specific function. You will need, for instance, a tool to make exact measurements, such as a wooden bench rule. You may also require the use of a folding wooden rule, often called a "zig-zag," or a retractable steel tape to measure and mark dimensions and larger spaces.

You will need tools that cut and shape material, such as hand saws, utility knives or a plane. The more complicated your unit, the larger the number of tools you will need from each category.

Depending on the method of construction used, you will need some type of fastener to hold pieces together. The plans may call for the use of nails, screws, bolts, glue or putty on various parts of the structure. In addition, you may need a hand or power drill to make the holes you will fit these fasteners in.

The instructions included with each pre-fab kit sometimes, but not always, list the tools required for the job. Also, some of the other plans available for homemade greenhouses list the tools you will need. Others do not. Each of the plans in this book, however, includes a list of the tools necessary to build the unit.

If you are still uncertain about which tools you will need after reading the instructions of your pre-fab kit, get in touch with the manufacturer or their representative and ask for their advice. Or, better yet, for advice on the tools needed for either a pre-fab or homemade greenhouse, ask a friend with experience in tools and a knowledge of construction techniques.

If you do not have much experience with tools, buy a pre-fab kit that the manufacturer specifies can be assembled using a small number of basic tools (hammer, saw, hand or power drill). Or be content with building an uncomplicated greenhouse from raw materials. The majority of the plans given in this book have been designed for a person having relatively little experience with tools or construction techniques. We have tried to make these plans as non-threatening and clear as possible, so that even if you have never built anything with your hands before, you should be able to construct one of these units by following the plan.

Don't attempt to build a unit requiring the skilled use of a wide variety of tools, and a detailed knowledge of construction, unless you already possess that skill and that knowledge. Or, if you are intent on building a large, complex structure, but you just don't have the background to know how to do the work, recruit a friend who has sufficient experience with tools, work materials and building rather large structures. You can waste considerable amounts of time, energy and money by jumping into a project that you simply cannot yet handle.

Many people are familiar with hand tools, and have some experience with using them. Others, like myself, initially view the subject as something of a mystery. This review of the tools needed in greenhouse construction, and their functions, is written with the uncertain tool-user in mind. In the course of building my own window unit greenhouse I found that patience and common sense, combined with the suggestions of a knowledgable friend, compensated for my initial lack of extensive experience. There is no mystery to tool use, if you follow a few basic rules. And the more you use a tool, the better at using it you should become.

If you are already familiar with tools, skip the next few pages and go on to the chapters on greenhouse construction. If you are unfamiliar with them, use this chapter as the first step in getting acquainted. It is not intended to be a complete introduction to the subject. The purpose of this chapter is to get you moving in the right direction, with greater confidence. After you have read the following, I suggest you consult one of the introductory books on tool use listed in the bibliography.

Don't abandon your hopes of a homemade greenhouse because you lack familiarity with tools. What you need to know to build, say, a window unit, you can learn. And once you have done it, you may discover, as I did, that you are anxious to go on to other, perhaps more complex, projects.

ABRASIVES

Abrasives, such as sandpaper, are used to achieve a smooth, regular surface on a piece of board or other material.

Sandpaper consists of a piece of thick, tough paper or cloth which is coated with glue. Particles of garnet, quartz or flint are sprinkled on the glue, in varying densities. Garnet paper is quite versatile, and can be used with good effect on wood.

Sandpaper is ranked in grades, ranging from very fine to very coarse. A paper having a low number is quite coarse. The higher the number, the finer the paper.

Because there are so many different kinds of sandpaper, you might find it worthwhile to ask about the qualities and uses of particular types when you shop for a supply.

Sandpaper is rubbed across a surface to remove irregularities, and when used on wood it is always rubbed with — not across or against — the grain of the wood.

CIRCULAR SAW

A circular power saw can save you time and effort if you must cut a large amount of wood for a project. Such saws are described by the size of their blade. A 7'' power saw (saw with a 7'' blade) should prove adequate for most home projects. However, unless you plan on doing quite a lot of woodwork, several hand saws may be all you need. Or perhaps you could borrow a circular saw, as well as get some advice on how to use it, from a neighbor.

When you use a power saw, keep a firm grip on it, and keep your free hand away from it. Make sure the board you are cutting is held firmly in place, so that there is no chance of it or the saw slipping. Start the saw before it touches the board, and guide it straight across on the outside of the line. Keep an especially firm grip on the saw at the end of a cut, so that it will not drop or jump as it slices through the last of the board.

Another attractive feature of the power saw is the variety of blades available. A combination crosscut and rip blade can be used for most jobs; an abrasive blade can be used on metal or masonry; a hollow ground blade will provide an exceptionally smooth, finished cut. In general, power saws provide a more accurate cut than a hand saw. But you must be alert when using one.

CHISEL

A Chisel is a type of knife used to make cuts in wood, removing chips or whole sections of a boards surface. A chisel consists of a steel blade, fastened to a plastic or wooden handle. The size of a chisel is determined by the width of the blade's cutting edge.

For superficial cuts in softwoods, the chisel is operated by hand pressure. However, for more extensive work with softwoods, and when used on hardwoods, a mallet of soft-faced hammer is used to tap the chisel along the wood. The handle of the chisel, held in one hand, is struck lightly by the mallet, held in the other hand, forcing the chisel along the wood in a short, regular stroke. Generally, the chisel is held in the left hand while the mallet is held in the right. The chisel must be held at a slight angle to the wood for greater control, so that the cut is light and does not gouge out uneven chunks.

36

HAMMER

Most of us have hefted a hammer at some point in our lives, even if only to speculatively pick it up and set it down. No matter whether you are assembling a pre-fab kit, or building a greenhouse from the ground up, you will need a hammer.

If you are working with wood, you will need a claw hammer. It is meant to be used only for driving and pulling nails. The claw of the hammer should be curved, so that you can remove nails. A straight claw is best used for ripping apart boards. Look for a hammer with a bell-faced (convex) striking surface. If you slip and drive a nail in it an off-angle, the hammer's convex surface will leave less of an impression in the wood.

The best hammer heads are of drop-forged steel. I suggest that your first hammer should be a heavy hammer, because the heavier the hammer, the larger its striking face. And the larger the face, the easier it is to hit the nail. Also, a heavy hammer is less likely to bounce off something and accidently strike you.

Grasp a hammer near the tip of its handle. Hold the nail between your thumb and forefinger, positioning it exactly where you want to drive it into the wood. Push it into the wood, tapping it lightly until it stands erect. You should hold the nail just below its head, and not at the surface of the wood. If you miss the nail, or if the nail folds up, the hammer will brush your fingers out of the way before it hits the wood, saving you some sore fingers.

Make certain the nail is centered and is not loose. Take your fingers, keep your eye on the head of the nail and hit it with force. Don't stand at an angle — try to bring the hammer down exactly on the head, and not just a part of the head. Hitting the nail hard reduces the chance of damaging your work, for the nail will be driven through too quickly to tear the wood. A nail struck softly at the wrong angle can splinter the wood. Indeed, even striking a nail softly at the right angle can be trouble, for "the friction bond between the wood and the nail will not be broken, so that the nail will pull the wood with it and break the wood."

Don't use a claw hammer for metal work. Use a ball peen hammer. A claw hammer might not have a face strong enough for some types of metal, and you risk shattering the face and harming yourself by using the wrong hammer for the job.

HAND DRILL

The hand drill is used to drill small holes rapidly — most often in wood. The drill generally consists of a handle, and a removable bit which is rotated and bores into the surface of a board. Start a hole by making an impression with an awl (a small, pointed hand punch), then use a drill. Hold the drill in a vertical position as you press down on the handle, or rotate it, or the hole will be too wide.

POWER DRILL

SCREWDRIVER

A power drill is a versatile and relatively inexpensive tool. It can make holes more rapidly — and with much less effort on your part — than can a hand-operated drill. In addition, it can be used with various accessories for sanding, grinding, buffing, polishing and other tasks.

Most drills can accept a variety of bits, allowing you to make holes of many sizes. Drills have "pistol-type" handles, and a trigger switch to set the bit in motion.

Before you drill, mark the location of the hole with a pencil dot or several intersecting lines. The drill bit often has a tendency to move off of the intended spot. Punch a small hole in the spot with an awl, to provide a seat for the bit. Don't turn the drill on until you are in position. Give the drill enough pressure with your hand to keep it from jumping away, but don't press so hard as to stall the motor. The harder the material, the more pressure will be required.

Power drills can be used on many types of metal, as well as wood. If you are working with metal, try drilling a small "pilot" hole first. It will make your work easier and more accurate. A few drops of kerosene or oil on the drill bit will make the drilling easier.

A screwdriver is a deceptively simple yet remarkably useful tool. Once you begin working on projects around the house, you'll be surprised by how often you reach for the screwdriver. Yet it has but one purpose: to drive in — and to draw out — screws used to join pieces of wood or metal together. Even the easier pre-fab greenhouse kits require a screwdriver for assembly.

Screws are used on a project when pieces of metal must be joined, when a project requires more holding power than nails can supply, or when the possibility exists that the project will later be disassambled.

You must match your screwdriver to the size, and the design, of the screws you will be using. The screws, and the project, can be damaged by attempting to use just any screwdriver that comes to hand.

It's a good idea to start screw holes with an awl or a hand drill. Put the screw in the hole. Grip the handle of the screwdriver so that it rests firmly within your palm. The longer (and heavier) the screwdriver you use, the easier it is to twist the screw into its hole without having the tip of the screwdriver slip off the head of the screw. If you encounter much resistance in twisting the screw home, remove it and enlarge the hole.

PLIERS

Pliers are used to bend and shape metal wire and metal sheet. They have two moveable parts, resembling jaws and having serrated edges for a strong grip. They are used to grip, to fasten and to unfasten objects.

WRENCHES

Nuts and bolts are fasteners used to hold pre-drilled metal sheets together. They are applied to the metal with a wrench. Wrenches can be used to hold, fasten and loosen nuts and bolts.

When you are fastening nuts and bolts, use a wrench that holds them without slipping off. Using a wrench that is too big for the job can damage and jam a nut, and the wrench might slip while you are working and slam into you.

Never use pliers to fasten nuts, because the edges of its "jaws" will mangle a nut. Once a damaged nut is in place, it will be difficult to remove it.

PLANE

A plane is a tool used to smooth the surfaces of rough cut wood. It has a blade fitted into a slot in a flat guide. The blade may be adjusted to extend at different lengths. The flat guide of a plane ensures that the blade will take a controlled bite of the surface to be smoothed. Too deep of a bite would only tear uneven chunks out of the surface. By moving a plane firmly and smoothly across the wood, long, uniform ribbons of wood will be sheared off. You can plane **with** the grain of a piece of wood, or across it, but never **against** it.

The piece of wood to be planed must be held securely by clamps, a vice or some other arrangement, so that it will not slip. Use both hands to bring steady downward pressure on the plane and to firmly guide it. Test the surface after you have finished to be certain that it has an equal flatness.

By planing, you create the flat, even board surfaces you must have for accurate construction.

WOOD SAW

Hand saws are used to cut all types of wood. To build a greenhouse, or even to assemble a pre-fab, you will need a saw.

On the board to be cut, pencil in a line to indicate where the cut is to be made. Begin by pulling the saw towards you, so that a small slot is cut in the edge of the board for the first downward stroke. Remember that a saw has a thickness of its own. Begin sawing on the **outside** of the line you have drawn, or you will end with a piece that is slightly too narrow. You can always plane away any excess left after cutting in this manner.

Draw the saw up carefully, slowly along the slot where you will begin. Repeat the initial upward motion several times. Then push down on the saw. Be sure to hold the saw firmly. You will needlessly tire yourself, and go off the line, by holding a saw loosely. Also, hold the wood firmly near where you are sawing with your other hand. But watch your fingers! Push down and bring the saw back up with a firm, steady movement. Put pressure on each downstroke, then bring the blade back up.

If there is resistance, make a number of short strokes. Don't force the blade. As you near the end of the cut, shorten the stroke and provide support for the severed pieces. As you saw, keep your fingers away from the blade, and concentrate on your movements.

Chapter 8.

FOUNDATIONS

FOUNDATIONS

Many books on home greenhouses try to avoid any detailed discussion of foundations. The reason for their evident uneasiness is quite simple — the cost of installing a foundation, or of having one installed, can send the total cost of your unit skyrocketing. While many books conclude that you must have a foundation, they shy away from stating just how much it will cost. It **can** be prohibitively expensive. And it has been my experience, at least, that it is becoming increasingly difficult to find a contractor who will handle what is to them a small job.

It is my belief that it is not absolutely necessary to install a foundation for a unit of 10' or less in length. Many greenhouse manufacturers seem to agree, as I have noticed an increasing number of pre-fab units on the market that require no foundation. Alternate, inexpensive methods have been worked out for anchoring and supporting a unit. The idea of building your own unit is to greatly reduce costs, but you can't do that if you must create an elaborate foundation. You aren't building for the ages, right? And I have seen no evidence that erecting a unit with some alternative to a foundation will decrease the practical number of years of use you can get out of a unit.

If you are determined to install a foundation, there are several texts on the subject listed in the bibliography. You will find one method of excavating a foundation illustrated here. In addition, you will find several illustrations for alternate methods of securing a unit — methods that are both simpler and less expensive.

FOUNDATION (*TRADITIONAL*)

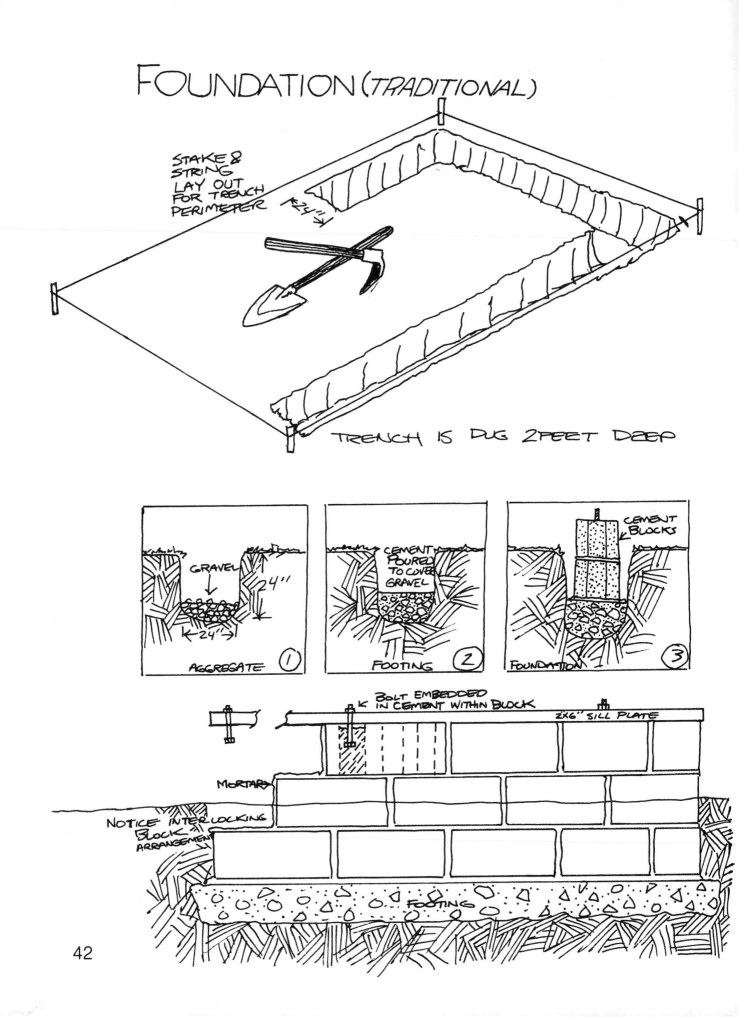

STAKE & STRING LAY OUT FOR TRENCH PERIMETER

←24"→

TRENCH IS DUG 2 FEET DEEP

GRAVEL

24"

24"

AGGREGATE ①

CEMENT POURED TO COVER GRAVEL

FOOTING ②

CEMENT BLOCKS

FOUNDATION ③

BOLT EMBEDDED IN CEMENT WITHIN BLOCK

2x6" SILL PLATE

MORTAR

NOTICE INTERLOCKING BLOCK ARRANGEMENT

FOOTING

SLAB FOUNDATION TECHNIQUE
(SEE PLANS CHAPTER FOR ALTERNATIVES TO FOUNDATIONS)

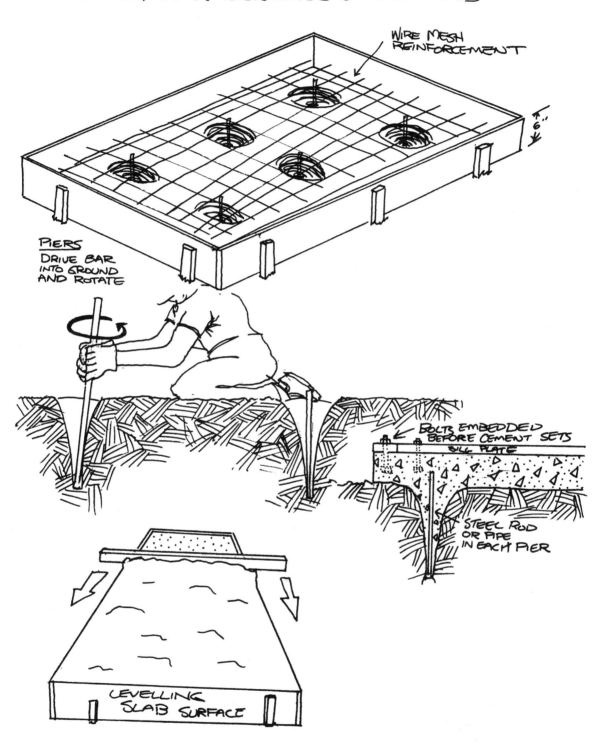

WIRE MESH REINFORCEMENT

6"

PIERS
DRIVE BAR INTO GROUND AND ROTATE

BOLTS EMBEDDED BEFORE CEMENT SETS
SILL PLATE

STEEL ROD OR PIPE IN EACH PIER

LEVELLING SLAB SURFACE

Chapter 9.

DESIGNS

You've selected a location for your greenhouse. You've decided on the size and style of your unit. Now where do you go for plans?

You can start right here. This chapter contains complete plans for six different greenhouses, all of them sharing an important characteristic — simplicity. These plans have been designed with the novice builder in mind. Any of these units can be built with a small number of familiar tools. None of them, with the possible exceptions of the dome and rigid frame units, should take more than several days to build.

The three window unit designs in this chapter are both simple and inexpensive. If you have never built anything before, or if you simply have no other space in which to build, I suggest constructing a window unit. These plans have been given without exact dimensions, so that you can adapt the units to the available space.

While dimensions have been given for the electrical conduit greenhouse, they can be altered according to your needs, so long as you keep the relationship of the parts in mind. Conduit is a very light but durable pipe available from electrical supply stores. Many stores will cut the pipe to the required lengths, if you bring them a list of the pieces and lengths required. They can also bend the pipe as it is required, and I suggest you have them do so. Trying to do

it yourself may leave you with several pieces of shattered conduit. Polyethylene plastic is used for the exterior of the unit. It can be purchased from building supply houses. The combination of conduit and plastic makes a light, but durable greenhouse. And you needn't build a large conduit unit. A smaller version of the unit can be constructed indoors, if you cannot build outdoors. A 4′ by 4′ greenhouse makes an unusual, but very practical addition, to a living room or family room. You can position the unit near your windows, or supplement sun light with fluorescent light.

The plan for the rigid frame greenhouse is drawn from a publication of the United States Department of Agriculture, prepared by the Cooperative Extension Service of the University of Illinois. While this design is not especially complex, it does require some familiarity with building procedures. If you can recruit a knowledgable friend to lend a hand, the plan should present no problem. It is included in this chapter because it is the simplest least expensive plan for a **large** greenhouse, aside from the conduit design, that I have ever seen.

The dome is not difficult — but it's design **is** quite unusual. I suggest that you approach it experimentally, taking time to work out each part of its construction beforehand, until the plan seems to hold no further mysteries. You'll be surprised, once you've mastered it, how simple it has become.

Window Greenhouse #1

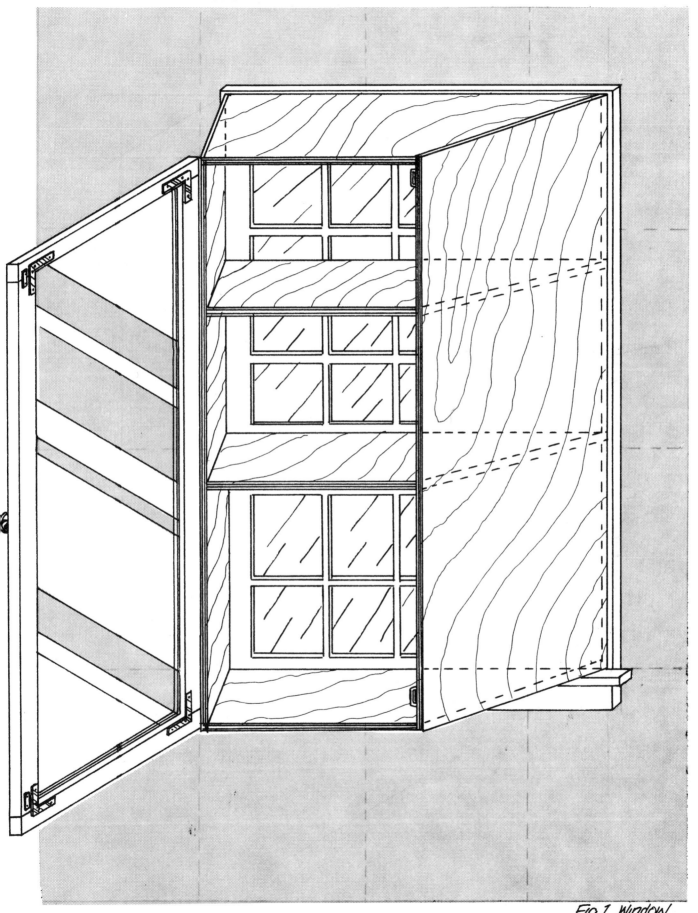

Fig.1. Window
GREENHOUSE #1

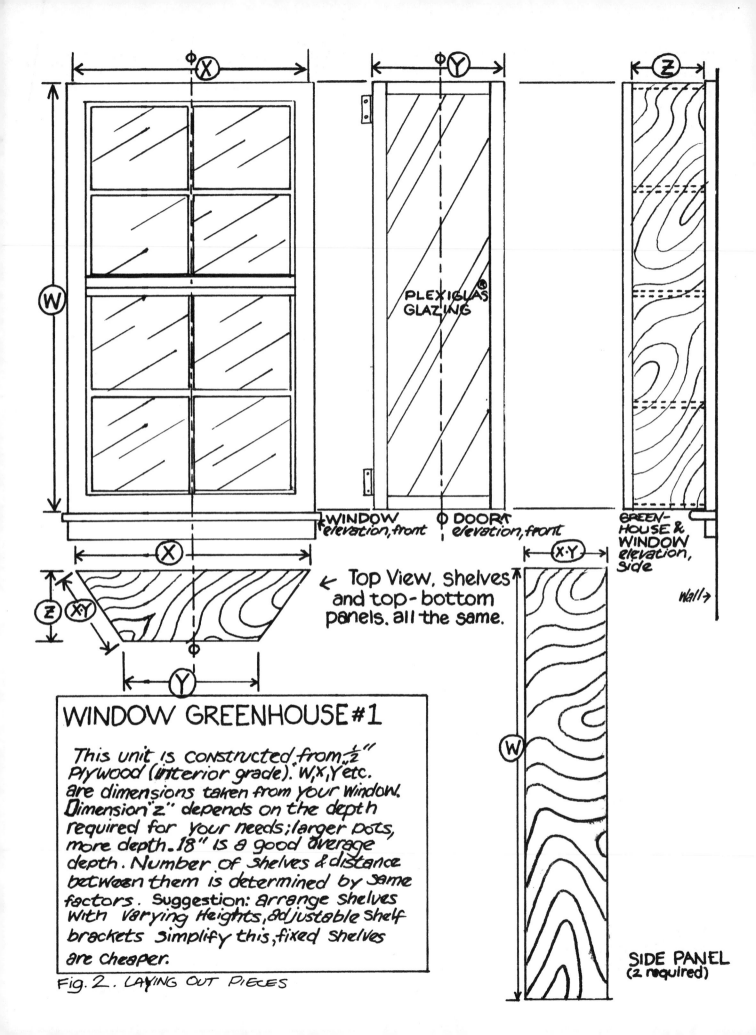

ⓍX

ⓎY

ⓏZ

Ⓦ W

PLEXIGLAS®
GLAZING

WINDOW
elevation, front

Ⓨ DOOR
elevation, front

GREEN-
HOUSE &
WINDOW
*elevation,
side*

Ⓧ X

ⓏZ Ⓧ·Ⓨ X·Y

Ⓨ Y

← Top View, shelves
and top-bottom
panels. all the same.

Ⓧ·Ⓨ X·Y

Ⓦ W

Wall →

WINDOW GREENHOUSE#1

*This unit is constructed from ½"
Plywood (interior grade). W,X,Y etc.
are dimensions taken from your Window.
Dimension "Z" depends on the depth
required for your needs; larger pots,
more depth. 18" is a good average
depth. Number of shelves & distance
between them is determined by same
factors. Suggestion: arrange shelves
with varying heights, adjustable shelf
brackets simplify this, fixed shelves
are cheaper.*

Fig. 2. LAYING OUT PIECES

SIDE PANEL
(2 required)

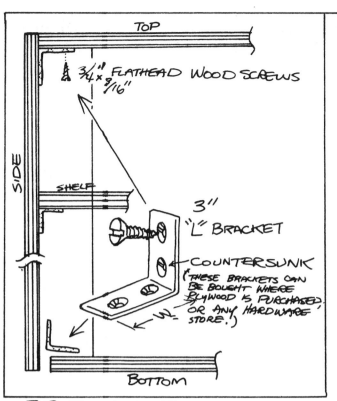

TOP

SIDE

$\frac{3}{4}$" × $\frac{9}{16}$" FLATHEAD WOOD SCREWS

SHELF

3" "L" BRACKET

COUNTERSUNK

(THESE BRACKETS CAN BE BOUGHT WHERE PLYWOOD IS PURCHASED, OR ANY HARDWARE STORE.)

W

BOTTOM

TOP-TO-SIDE FASTENING
(BACK VIEW)

HINGE

← DOOR

SIDE

UNDERSIDE OF TOP

"L" BRACKETS

NOTE:

THE USE OF "L" BRACKETS IS SHOWN HERE, BECAUSE IT IS THE SIMPLEST WAY OF DOING THE JOB.
IF YOU SAY, "WHY, I KNOW A BETTER WAY OF DOING THAT JOB," YOU'LL PROBABLY BE RIGHT. YOU'LL ALSO PROBABLY HAVE THE SKILLS TO DO IT.

TOP-TO-SIDE FASTENING
(BOTTOM VIEW)

TOP

TOP PIECE ALLOWANCE ½"

TO LAYOUT "L" BRACKET MOUNTING HOLES, PLACE SIDE PANELS TOGETHER SIDE-BY-SIDE. THIS ALLOWS FOR ACCURATE HOLE POSITION- ING, AND KEEPS BOTH PIECES IDENTICAL. BE SURE TO ALLOW FOR TOP & BOTTOM PIECES AS SHOWN IN DRAWING. AFTER DRAWING LINES, DRILL OR DRIVE NAIL FOR PILOT HOLES. THIS MAKES DRIVING SCREWS EASIER & MORE ACCURATE. BE SURE TO MAKE PILOT HOLE SMALLER THAN DIAMETER OF SCREW THREADS.

INSIDE LEFT SIDE

INSIDE RIGHT SIDE

BOTTOM

ALLOWANCE FOR BOTTOM PIECE ½"

MOUNTING TOP & SHELVES TO SIDES.
Fig 3. WINDOW greenhouse #1

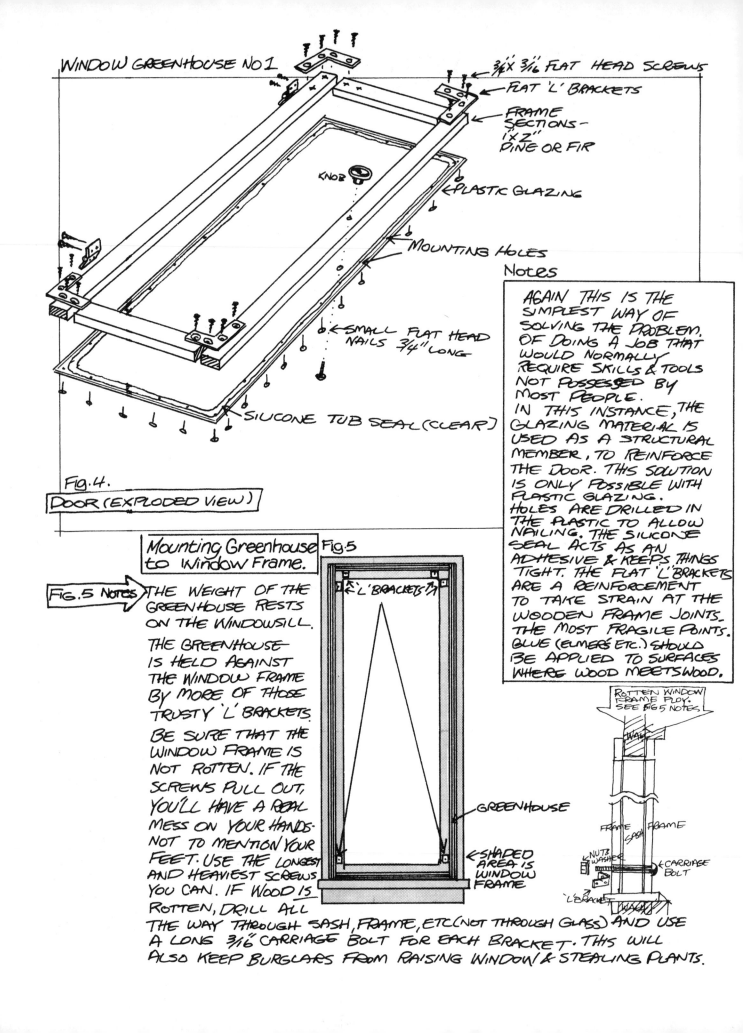

WINDOW GREENHOUSE NO 1

3/4" X 3/16" FLAT HEAD SCREWS

FLAT 'L' BRACKETS

FRAME SECTIONS - 1"X 2" PINE OR FIR

KNOB

PLASTIC GLAZING

MOUNTING HOLES

SMALL FLAT HEAD NAILS 3/4" LONG

SILICONE TUB SEAL (CLEAR)

Fig.4.

Door (EXPLODED VIEW)

Notes

AGAIN THIS IS THE SIMPLEST WAY OF SOLVING THE PROBLEM. OF DOING A JOB THAT WOULD NORMALLY REQUIRE SKILLS & TOOLS NOT POSSESSED BY MOST PEOPLE.
IN THIS INSTANCE, THE GLAZING MATERIAL IS USED AS A STRUCTURAL MEMBER, TO REINFORCE THE DOOR. THIS SOLUTION IS ONLY POSSIBLE WITH PLASTIC GLAZING. HOLES ARE DRILLED IN THE PLASTIC TO ALLOW NAILING. THE SILICONE SEAL ACTS AS AN ADHESIVE & KEEPS THINGS TIGHT. THE FLAT 'L' BRACKETS ARE A REINFORCEMENT TO TAKE STRAIN AT THE WOODEN FRAME JOINTS. THE MOST FRAGILE POINTS. GLUE (ELMERS ETC.) SHOULD BE APPLIED TO SURFACES WHERE WOOD MEETS WOOD.

Mounting Greenhouse to Window Frame. Fig. 5

Fig. 5 Notes → THE WEIGHT OF THE GREENHOUSE RESTS ON THE WINDOWSILL.

THE GREENHOUSE IS HELD AGAINST THE WINDOW FRAME BY MORE OF THOSE TRUSTY 'L' BRACKETS

BE SURE THAT THE WINDOW FRAME IS NOT ROTTEN. IF THE SCREWS PULL OUT, YOU'LL HAVE A REAL MESS ON YOUR HANDS. NOT TO MENTION YOUR FEET. USE THE LONGEST AND HEAVIEST SCREWS YOU CAN. IF WOOD IS ROTTEN, DRILL ALL THE WAY THROUGH SASH, FRAME, ETC (NOT THROUGH GLASS) AND USE A LONG 3/16" CARRIAGE BOLT FOR EACH BRACKET. THIS WILL ALSO KEEP BURGLARS FROM RAISING WINDOW & STEALING PLANTS.

'L' BRACKETS

GREENHOUSE

SHADED AREA IS WINDOW FRAME

ROTTEN WINDOW FRAME PLOY. SEE FIG 5 NOTES

WALL

FRAME FRAME
SASH

NUT & WASHER

CARRIAGE BOLT

'L' BRACKET

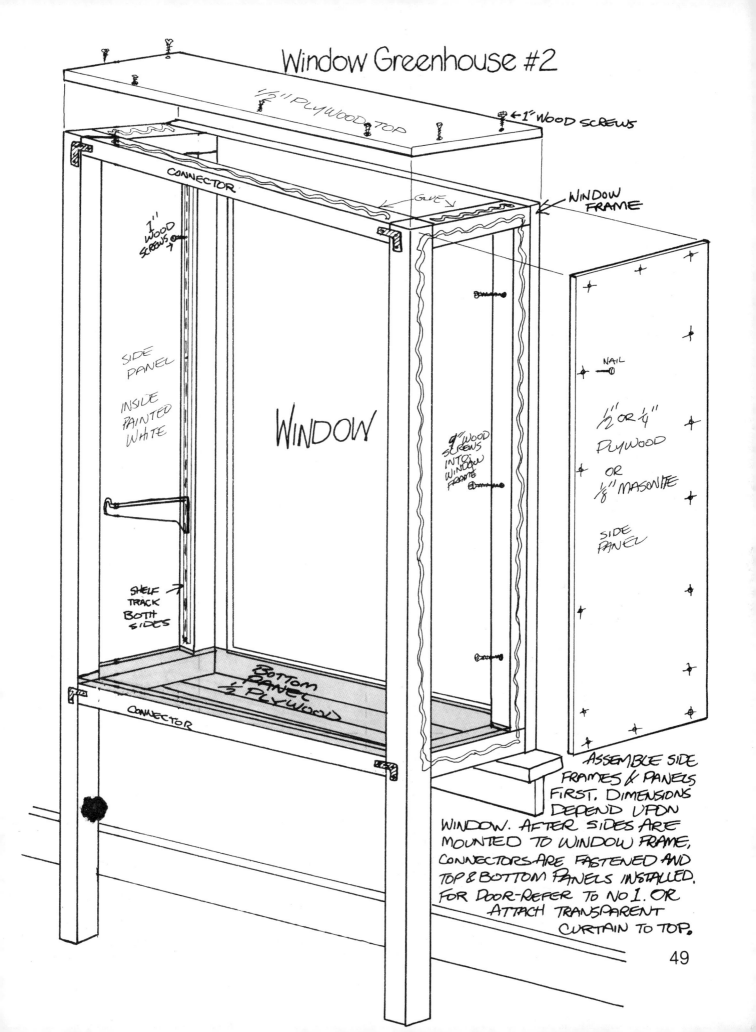

Window Greenhouse #2

½" PLYWOOD TOP

← 1" WOOD SCREWS

CONNECTOR

GLUE

WINDOW FRAME

1" WOOD SCREWS

SIDE PANEL

INSIDE PAINTED WHITE

WINDOW

NAIL

1" WOOD SCREWS INTO WINDOW FRAME

½" OR ¼" PLYWOOD

OR

⅛" MASONITE

SIDE PANEL

SHELF TRACK BOTH SIDES

BOTTOM PANEL ½" PLYWOOD

CONNECTOR

ASSEMBLE SIDE FRAMES & PANELS FIRST. DIMENSIONS DEPEND UPON WINDOW. AFTER SIDES ARE MOUNTED TO WINDOW FRAME, CONNECTORS ARE FASTENED AND TOP & BOTTOM PANELS INSTALLED. FOR DOOR-REFER TO NO.1. OR ATTACH TRANSPARENT CURTAIN TO TOP.

49

Window Greenhouse #3
TEN DOLLAR SPECIAL

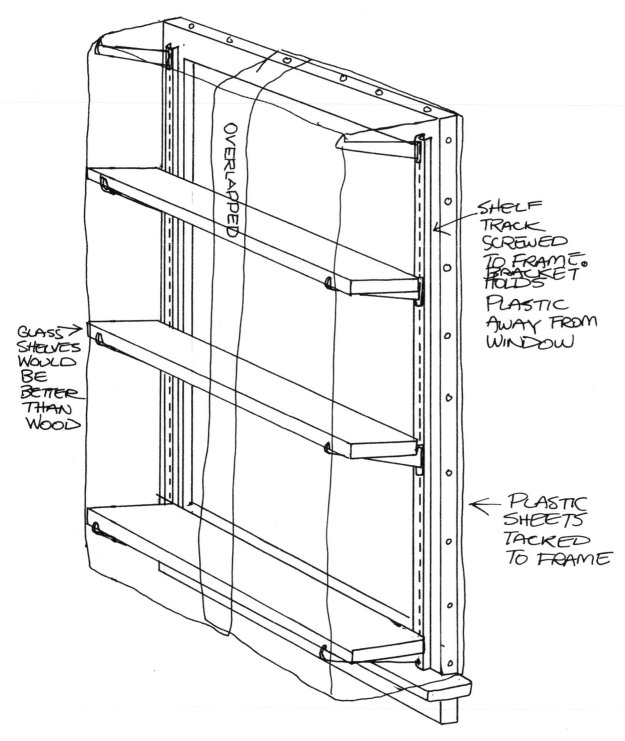

OVERLAPPED

SHELF TRACK SCREWED TO FRAME. BRACKET HOLDS PLASTIC AWAY FROM WINDOW

GLASS SHELVES WOULD BE BETTER THAN WOOD

PLASTIC SHEETS TACKED TO FRAME

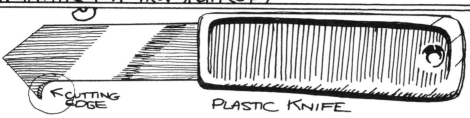

Cutting Plastics

PLASTIC KNIFE

CUTTING EDGE

PLASTIC SHEET

METAL STRAIGHT EDGE

PULL

TABLE EDGE

THE PLASTIC KNIFE IS A RELATIVELY NEW TOOL. AS SOON AS I SAW THE FIRST ONES ON THE MARKET TWO YEARS AGO, I COULDN'T GET THE MONEY OUT OF MY POCKET FAST ENOUGH. IT REALLY WORKS WELL, ESPECIALLY FOR GLAZING-TYPE PLASTICS. THIS KNIFE IS TO PLASTIC WHAT A GLASS-CUTTING WHEEL IS TO GLASS, AND ITS SIMPLER TO USE. IT CUTS PLEXIGLAS® FIBERGLASS, BAKELITE AND JUST ABOUT ANY-THING SIMILAR.

WHERE TO BUY IT:

TRY HARDWARE STORES, CRAFT SUPPLY HOUSE, LUMBER YARDS OR PLASTICS DISTRIBUTORS.

How to use the Plastic Knife:

AFTER DETERMINING WHERE CUT IS TO BE MADE, PLACE STRAIGHTEDGE ALONG LINE (AT FIRST, YOU SHOULD USE METAL. AFTER YOUR SKILL IM-PROVES, YOU CAN GET AWAY WITH A WOODEN YARDSTICK.) THE KNIFE DOES ITS CUTTING ON A PULL STROKE; SO, ITS DRAWN TOWARD YOU, GUIDED BY THE STRAIGHTEDGE. NOTICE THAT THE NEAR EDGE OF THE PLASTIC OVERHANGS THE WORK SURFACE SLIGHTLY. THIS IS BECAUSE OF THE FOLLOW-THROUGH NECESSARY FOR THE CUT. IF YOU STOP AT THE EDGE, THE SCORE WON'T BE DEEP ENOUGH AND YOU'LL HAVE AN UNEVEN BREAK.

THE FIRST PASS OF THE BLADE SHOULD BE DONE VERY LIGHTLY AND SMOOTHLY. SUCCESSIVE PASSES ARE DONE WITH INCREASING PRESSURE, UNTIL THE SCORE IS APPROX. 1/3 THROUGH THE THICKNESS OF THE SHEET.

AT THIS POINT, THE SCORE IS PLACED OVER THE WORK SURFACE EDGE. THE OPEN PALM OF YOUR HAND IS THEN SLAPPED SMARTLY AGAINST THE OVERHANGING SECTION. (YELLING EEEYAH!! IS OPTIONAL.) THE PLASTIC SNAPS WITH A SHARP CRACK, USUALLY LANDING ON YOUR FOOT. SHOES ARE A GOOD IDEA.

Note: the Whole Process Actually takes less time than reading these directions. It's also a lot of fun. The same process applies to building plastic furniture, so your Greenhouse can be good practice.

ELECTRICAL CONDUIT GREENHOUSE *for indoor or outdoor use*

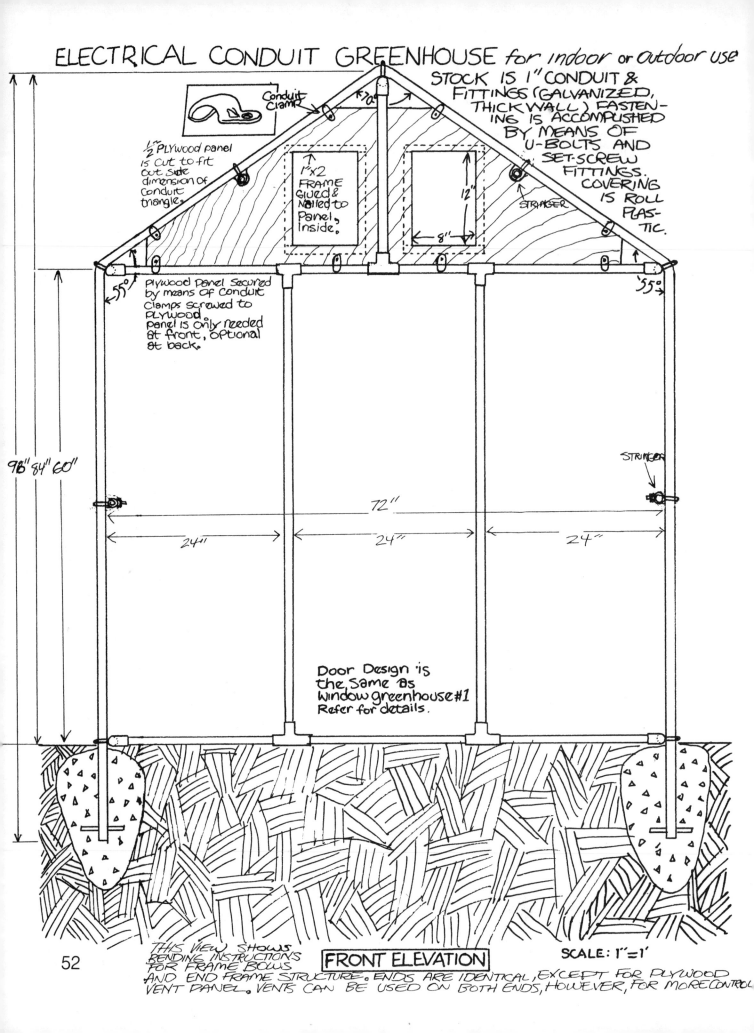

STOCK IS 1" CONDUIT & FITTINGS (GALVANIZED, THICK WALL) FASTENING IS ACCOMPLISHED BY MEANS OF U-BOLTS AND SET-SCREW FITTINGS. COVERING IS ROLL PLASTIC.

Conduit Clamp

1/2" PLYWOOD panel is cut to fit out side dimension of conduit triangle.

1"x2" FRAME Glued & Nailed to Panel, Inside.

12"

8"

STRINGER

55°   55°

Plywood panel secured by means of conduit clamps screwed to PLYWOOD. panel is only needed at front, optional at back.

STRINGER

96" 84" 60"

72"

24"   24"   24"

Door Design is the same as Window greenhouse #1. Refer for details.

52

THIS VIEW SHOWS BENDING INSTRUCTIONS FOR FRAME BOWS AND END FRAME STRUCTURE. ENDS ARE IDENTICAL, EXCEPT FOR PLYWOOD VENT PANEL. VENTS CAN BE USED ON BOTH ENDS, HOWEVER, FOR MORE CONTROL

FRONT ELEVATION

SCALE: 1" = 1'

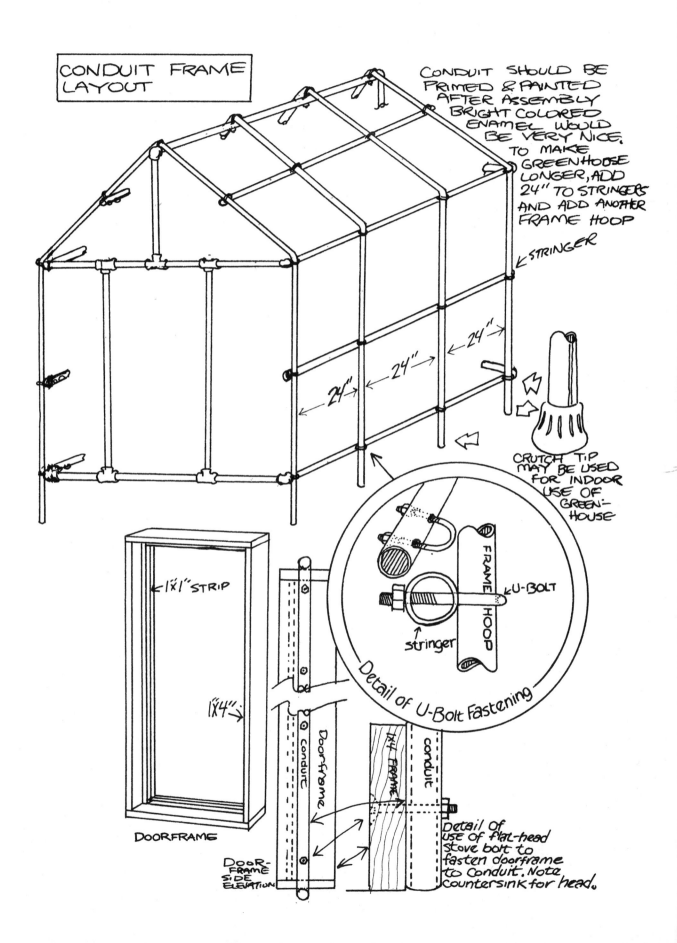

CONDUIT FRAME LAYOUT

CONDUIT SHOULD BE PRIMED & PAINTED AFTER ASSEMBLY BRIGHT COLORED ENAMEL WOULD BE VERY NICE. TO MAKE GREENHOUSE LONGER, ADD 24" TO STRINGERS AND ADD ANOTHER FRAME HOOP

←STRINGER

24"   24"   ←24"

CRUTCH TIP MAY BE USED FOR INDOOR USE OF GREEN-HOUSE

←1"x1" STRIP

1"x4"

DOORFRAME

Detail of U-Bolt Fastening

FRAME HOOP

←U-BOLT

↑ stringer

Door-frame

Door-FRAME SIDE ELEVATION

conduit

1x4 FRAME

conduit

Detail of use of flat-head stove bolt to fasten doorframe to Conduit. Note countersink for head.

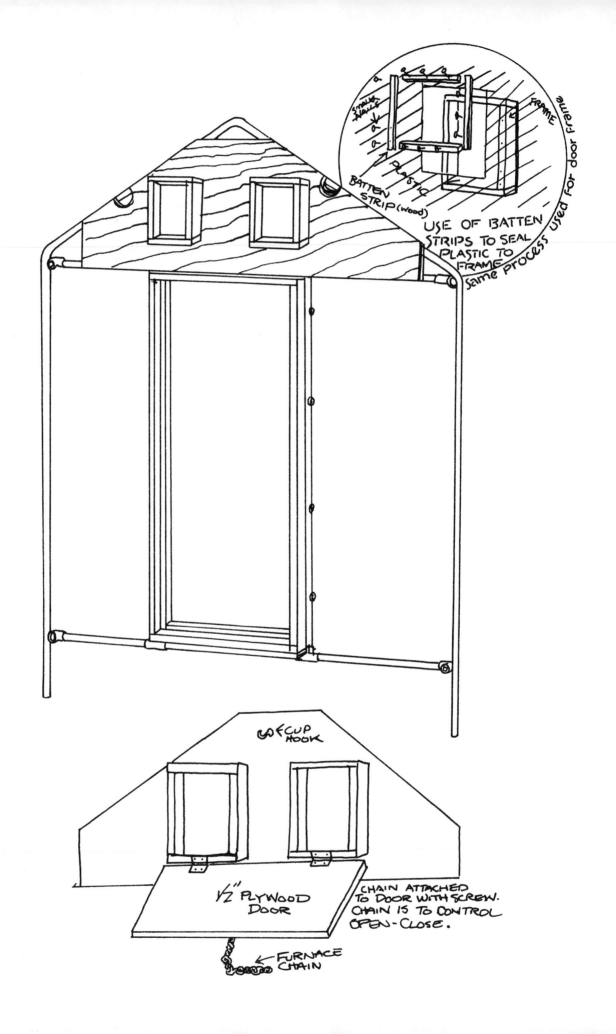

USE OF BATTEN STRIPS TO SEAL PLASTIC TO FRAME

BATTEN STRIP (wood)

FRAME

PLASTIC

STAPLES/NAILS

Same Process used for door Frame

CUP HOOK

1/2" PLYWOOD DOOR

CHAIN ATTACHED TO DOOR WITH SCREW. CHAIN IS TO CONTROL OPEN-CLOSE.

← FURNACE CHAIN

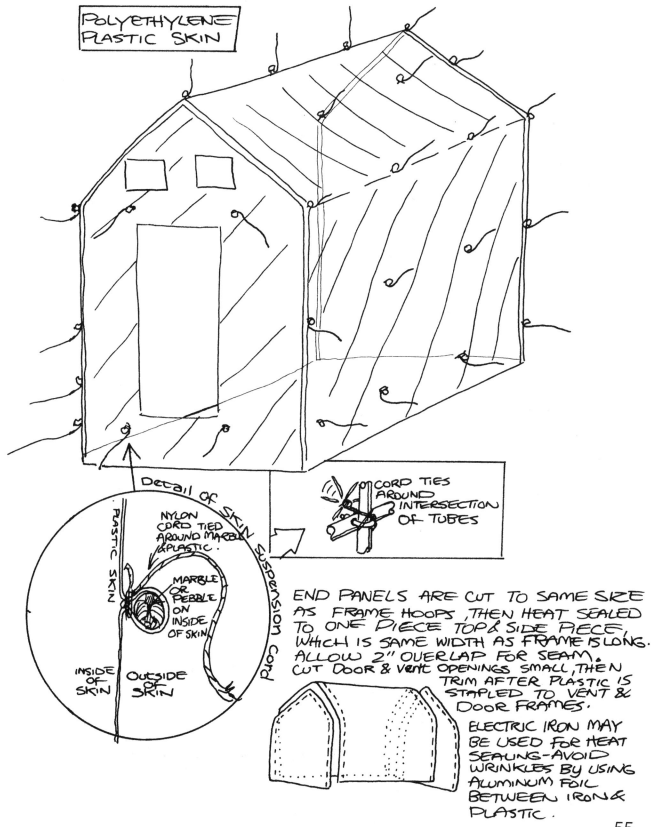

POLYETHYLENE PLASTIC SKIN

Detail of skin

PLASTIC SKIN

Suspension Cord

NYLON CORD TIED AROUND MARBLE & PLASTIC.

MARBLE OR PEBBLE ON INSIDE OF SKIN

INSIDE OF SKIN

OUTSIDE OF SKIN

CORD TIES AROUND INTERSECTION OF TUBES

END PANELS ARE CUT TO SAME SIZE AS FRAME HOOPS, THEN HEAT SEALED TO ONE PIECE TOP & SIDE PIECE, WHICH IS SAME WIDTH AS FRAME IS LONG. ALLOW 2" OVERLAP FOR SEAM. CUT DOOR & VENT OPENINGS SMALL, THEN TRIM AFTER PLASTIC IS STAPLED TO VENT & DOOR FRAMES.

ELECTRIC IRON MAY BE USED FOR HEAT SEALING - AVOID WRINKLES BY USING ALUMINUM FOIL BETWEEN IRON & PLASTIC.

55

A SIMPLE RIGID FRAME GREENHOUSE

MAXIMUM 36" ON CENTER

NOTE: HOUSE MAY BE
BUILT ANY DESIRED
LENGTH WITH FRAMES
SPACED UP TO 36" O.C.

Covering. This greenhouse is designed for covering with rigid fiberglass panels or with film plastics such as weatherable vinyl, or inexpensive polyethylene. Construction of the framing is slightly different for corrugated fiberglass than for flat fiberglass and the film plastics see plan

Building the frames. The rigid frames are made of 2″ x 4″ construction grade fir lumber (or other grades and species having equal strength). A jig or pattern forming the dimensions given in the plan (center fold) can be made by nailing boards to a wooden floor, plywood sheets, or to other boards. The 2″ x 4″ members are then cut and fitted in the jig. The frames are made rigid by gluing and nailing ⅜″ AC exterior-grade plywood gussets over the joints (Fig. 1). Resorcinol-resin glue, which is waterproof and which sets under low pressure at normal air temperatures, is recommended for greenhouse construction. The frames should be stored level for 24 hours after nailing and gluing the gussets. A complete frame can be made from two 10-foot 2″ x 4″ members.

Size of greenhouse. The frames should be spaced according to the width and kind of the plastic to be used, but not wider than 36″ on center. Frames can be spaced 32 inches on center for 34-inch wide corrugated fiberglass, or 36 inches on center for polyethylene, vinyl, or flat fiberglass. Convenient greenhouse sizes for these frame spacings are 10′ x 10′8″ (5 frames) or 10 x 15 (6 frames), respectively. The techniques described in this circular can be used to build frames for a lean-to greenhouse (half frames) or for a greenhouse of larger dimensions.

A rigid frame formed in a jig with plywood gussets being glued and nailed over the joints. Note the filler block which may be cut from a 2″ x 2″ (shown) or 2″ x 4″ member. Fourpenny nails secure the gussets until the glue dries. (Fig. 1)

Foundation. Two solid and inexpensive foundations are shown in the plan (center fold). The concrete foundation is recommended for a permanent, trouble-free installation (Fig. 2). Framing anchors or angle-iron braces attach the frames to the sill plate and foundation. Pieces cut 2½ inches wide from 2½- or 3-inch angle-iron and drilled for ⅜-inch bolts make excellent anchors.

Floor. A center walk can be made of concrete, flagstones, stepping stones, or pea-gravel and should be raised and sloped for run-off of water. Crushed rock or stones can be placed under the benches for neat appearance and to catch excess water.

Installation of plastic. The frames must be notched at the peak and eaves of the roof to receive continuous 1″ x 4″ members for film plastics or flat fiberglass (Fig. 3). One edge of the eave and peak members must be beveled to form a smooth corner surface for application of the plastic. This additional cutting and fitting is not necessary for installation of corrugated fiberglass (Fig. 4).

Film plastics (vinyl or polyethylene) are attached with painted 1″ x 2″ fir or redwood strips nailed to the frames (Fig. 3). Flat fiberglass can be attached with round-head screws backed with neoprene washers.

The roof can be easily covered with corrugated fiberglass by cutting 10-foot panels in half. This will allow a 3- to 4-inch overhang at the eave. Two 34-inch wide corrugated panels, installed horizontally with proper overlap, exactly covers one side. Special rubber or redwood closure strips are used to seal along the edges of the wall and roof (Fig. 4). Detailed installation instructions, available from fiberglass manufacturers and suppliers, should be obtained before construction. Flat, rather than corrugated fiberglass, may be used for easier covering of the ends.

Benches. The greenhouse is designed for two 30- to 36-inch wide benches. The plan shows how to construct supports for the bench shown in Fig. 5. A permanent bench to rest on the pipe supports can be made of cypress or redwood boards. Prefabricated benches made of asbestos cement (Fig. 5) or redwood are available from greenhouse supply companies.

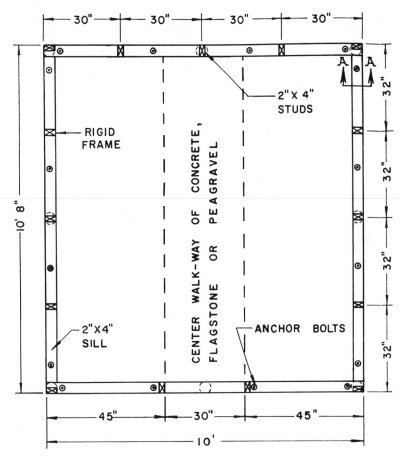

30"   30"   30"   30"

32"

2" X 4" STUDS

RIGID FRAME

32"

10' 8"

32"

CENTER WALK-WAY OF CONCRETE, FLAGSTONE OR PEAGRAVEL

32"

2" X 4" SILL

ANCHOR BOLTS

45"   30"   45"

10'

PLAN AND ELEVATION OF STRUCTURE ON CONCRETE

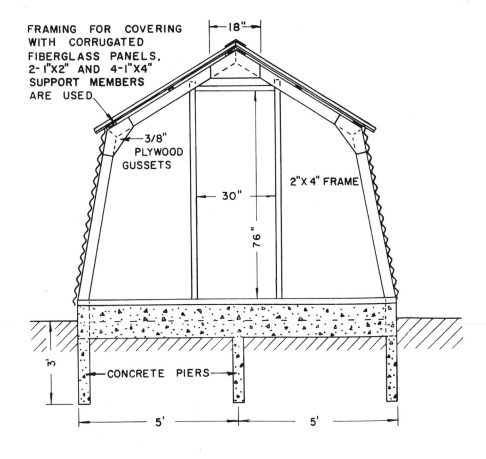

FRAMING FOR COVERING WITH CORRUGATED FIBERGLASS PANELS, 2-1"X2" AND 4-1"X4" SUPPORT MEMBERS ARE USED.

18"

3/8" PLYWOOD GUSSETS

30"

2" X 4" FRAME

76"

3'

CONCRETE PIERS

5'   5'

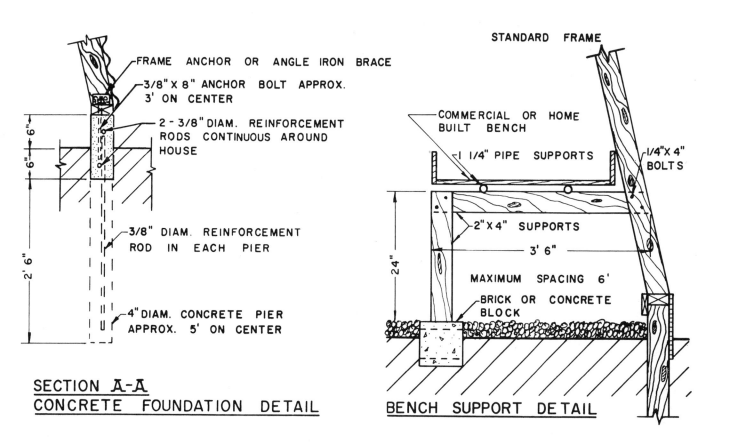

FRAME ANCHOR OR ANGLE IRON BRACE

3/8" X 8" ANCHOR BOLT APPROX. 3' ON CENTER

2 - 3/8" DIAM. REINFORCEMENT RODS CONTINUOUS AROUND HOUSE

3/8" DIAM. REINFORCEMENT ROD IN EACH PIER

4" DIAM. CONCRETE PIER APPROX. 5' ON CENTER

6"

6"

2' 6"

SECTION A-A
CONCRETE FOUNDATION DETAIL

STANDARD FRAME

COMMERCIAL OR HOME BUILT BENCH

1 1/4" PIPE SUPPORTS

1/4" X 4" BOLTS

2" X 4" SUPPORTS

3' 6"

24"

MAXIMUM SPACING 6'

BRICK OR CONCRETE BLOCK

BENCH SUPPORT DETAIL

FRONT ELEVATION AND DETAIL OF ALTERNATE FOUNDATION

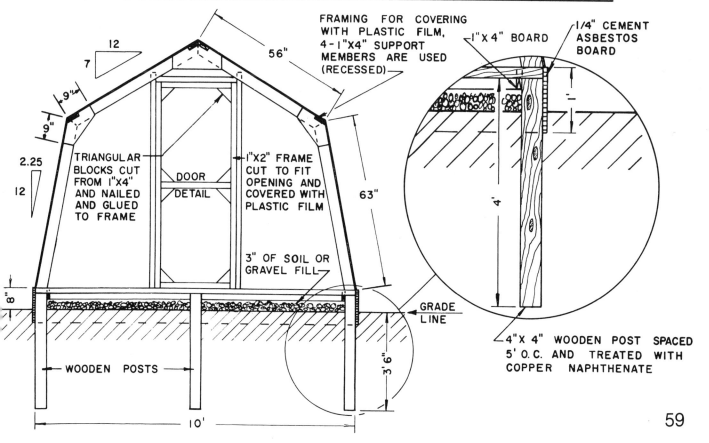

12
7

9"
9"

2.25
12

TRIANGULAR BLOCKS CUT FROM 1"X4" AND NAILED AND GLUED TO FRAME

DOOR DETAIL

56"

FRAMING FOR COVERING WITH PLASTIC FILM, 4-1"X4" SUPPORT MEMBERS ARE USED (RECESSED)

1"X2" FRAME CUT TO FIT OPENING AND COVERED WITH PLASTIC FILM

63"

3" OF SOIL OR GRAVEL FILL

8"

WOODEN POSTS

10'

GRADE LINE

3' 6"

1" X 4" BOARD

1/4" CEMENT ASBESTOS BOARD

4'

4"X 4" WOODEN POST SPACED 5' O.C. AND TREATED WITH COPPER NAPHTHENATE

59

Concrete foundation with sill ready for rigid frames. (Fig. 2)

The eaves of the roof, showing the notched frames. (Fig. 3)

The installation of corrugated fiberglass by means of wood screws and closure strips. (Fig. 4)

Asbestos cement benches for the greenhouse.   **(Fig. 5)**

Approximate Material Costs for a 10′ x 10′8″ Rigid Frame Home Greenhouse

Framing (lumber, glue, nails)...	$ 50-60
Plastic (including necessary fasteners)	
Fiberglass	125–175
Vinyl..	25–35
Polyethylene..	15–20
Foundation	
Post	15–25
Concrete...	30–50
Heater..	75–125
Ventilation fan (shutters, wall box, guard, thermostat).................	75–100
Benches (two 3′ x 10′, redwood or asbestos)...........................	50–75

Paint. All wooden framing members should be painted with a good white paint. Special greenhouse paint, which usually contains a fungicide, is preferable. Paints which give off toxic vapors, especially those containing mercury compounds, should be avoided.

Benches and wood members in or near the ground can be treated with a good wood preservative such as 2 percent copper naphthenate. Never use creosote or pentachlorophenol preservatives in a greenhouse.

Heating and ventilation. The greenhouse must be properly heated and ventilated for year-round enjoyment. Thermostatically controlled exhaust fans, rather than manual vents, are recommended for positive ventilation of this rigid frame home greenhouse. Refer to University of Illinois Circular 879, *Home Greenhouses,* for information on heaters for small greenhouses, amount of heat required, and ventilation.

Prepared by J. W. Courter, Associate Professor of Horticulture, and J. O. Curtis, Professor of Agricultural Engineering.

Urbana, Illinois   Revised, April, 1972

Issued in furtherance of Cooperative Extension Work, Acts of May 8 and June 30, 1914, in cooperation with the U.S. Department of Agriculture. JOHN B. CLAAR, *Director,* Cooperative Extension Service, University of Illinois at Urbana-Champaign.

Dome Greenhouse

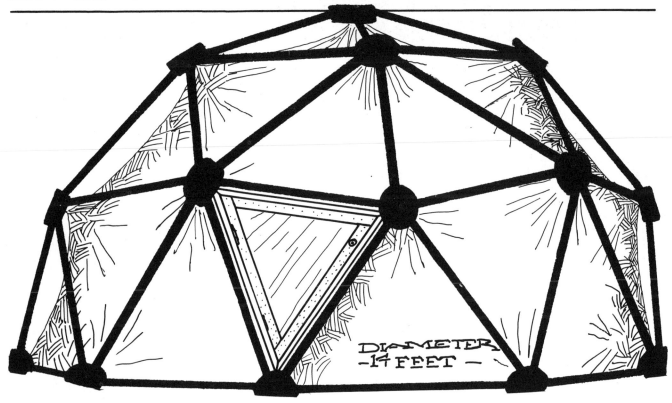

DIAMETER
—14 FEET —

Notes on Geodesic Dome Greenhouse—
CONSIDERING THE AMOUNT OF SPACE ENCLOSED, THIS GREENHOUSE IS PROBABLY THE CHEAPEST TO BUILD IN THE WHOLE BOOK. COST OF MATERIALS FOR FRAME, HUBS, AND SKIN IS LESS THAN 100 DOLLARS.

THERE <u>ARE</u> SOME DRAWBACKS TO THIS DESIGN, HOWEVER. AMONG THEM ARE : THESE GEODESICS CAN GET AWFULLY COMPLICATED, ESPECIALLY IF YOU TEND TO BE SLOPPY ABOUT MEASUREMENTS, SAWING, DRILLING ETC. THE PRINCIPLE THAT MAKES GEODESICS SO EFFICIENT IS THAT THE STRUCTURAL MEMBERS SUPPORT EACH OTHER IN A VERY INTRIGATE RELATIONSHIP. STRESS APPLIED TO ONE MEMBER IS TRANSFERRED TO AND SHARED BY THE OTHER MEMBERS. THE SAME GOES FOR ERRORS, EACH ERROR IS ADDED TO THE NEXT TO PRODUCE A TOTAL GREATER THAN THE INDIVIDUAL ERRORS. THIS IS NOT TRUE WITH MOST OTHER WAYS OF BUILDING STRUCTURES. A ¼" ERROR IN CUTTING A PIECE OF WOOD FOR A NORMAL TYPE OF GREENHOUSE ONLY AFFECTS THE OTHER PARTS THAT ARE INTIMATELY CONNECTED TO IT, IN A LOT OF CASES, IT WOULDN'T MATTER AT ALL. SUCH IS NOT THE CASE WITH A DOME.

CONT. →

HERES ANOTHER DRAWBACK:
THE DOOR WAY OF THIS DESIGN IS LIMITED TO THE
SIZE AND SHAPE OF ONE OF THE TRIANGLES. IN ORDER
TO HAVE A LARGER OPENING, ONE OR MORE STRUTS
WILL HAVE TO BE REMOVED. THIS WOULD SERIOUSLY WEAKEN
THE STRUCTURE, UNLESS ADDITIONAL REINFORCEMENT IS
USED AROUND THE OPENING. SO YOUR DOOR WOULD BE
TRIANGULAR AND ABOUT 48" PER SIDE. A RELATIVELY
SUPPLE PHYSIQUE IS A NECESSITY FOR THE USER, ALSO
GETTING TREES IN AND OUT WOULD BE A PROBLEM.
THERE WILL BE SKETCHES LATER ON TO SUGGEST OPTIONS,
HOWEVER.

ABOUT STRUTS:

STRUTS ARE CUT FROM 1" POLYETHELYNE
WATER PIPE. THIS IS A FLEXIBLE PIPE THAT
COMES IN ROLLS. A 300' ROLL IS SUFFICIENT
FOR THIS DESIGN. PRICE SHOULD BE $60-
$70 FOR THIS MUCH, IT'S AVAILABLE AT ANY
PLUMBING SUPPLY STORE PLUS SEARS, ETC.
THE NORMAL COLOR IS BLACK. THE FLEXABILITY
OF THE PIPE MAKES FOR A MUCH SIMPLER
DESIGN, AS THE STRUTS FORM A 17° ANGLE
WITH THE HUB. WITH A RIGID STRUT, THE
ANGLE WOULD HAVE TO BE DESIGNED INTO
EITHER THE STRUT OR THE HUB, THIS IS NOT
A PROBLEM AS THE STRUT WILL NATURALLY
TAKE ON THIS ANGLE IF IT CAN FLEX.

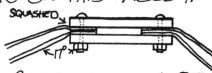

THE ACTUAL LENGTH OF THE STRUT IS
NOT CRITICAL, THE DISTANCE BETWEEN HOLES
IS. ANOTHER IMPORTANT FACTOR IS THAT
HOLES SHOULD BE PARALLEL (SEE BELOW)

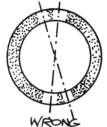 

IF THEY'RE NOT
THE STRUTS WILL
HAVE TO TWIST,
WHICH MAY SET
UP UNDESIRABLE
STRESSES. SLIGHT
VARIATIONS SHOULDN'T
BE A PROBLEM,
THOUGH.

AS YOU CAN SEE FROM THE DRAWINGS, THE STRUT
ENDS ARE SQUASHED BETWEEN THE HUB PLATES
BY THE CARRIAGE BOLTS, THIS MAKES THE BEND
SIMPLER. THEY DON'T HAVE TO BE SQUEEZED
ABSOLUTELY FLAT, THOUGH.

LONG
STRUT (L)
35 NEEDED

SHORT
STRUT (S)
30 NEEDED

1"

1"

51" 49"

45"

43"

1" 1"

63

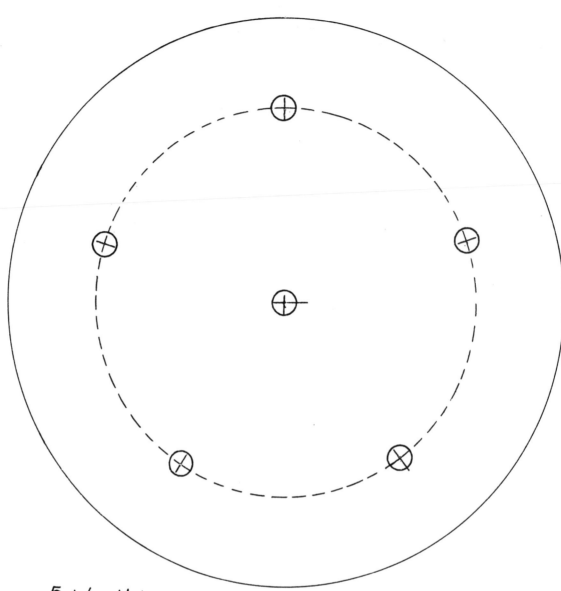

5-Way Hub
20 NEEDED (½"EXTERIOR PLYWOOD)

HUB NOTES NO. 2 —
THE HUB HOLES ARE MUCH MORE
IMPORTANT THAN THE SHAPE
OF THE HUB ITSELF, SO DON'T
THROW ONE AWAY JUST 'CAUSE
IT ISN'T PERFECTLY ROUND.
IF THE HOLES AREN'T RIGHT,
HOWEVER YOU'LL HAVE A PROB-
LEM BOLTING THE HUBS
TOGETHER. IF YOU HAVE
DIFFICULTY GETTING
ACCURACY, CLAMP 2 OF THEM
TOGETHER IN A SANDWICH,
AND DRILL THE PAIR AT
THE SAME TIME.

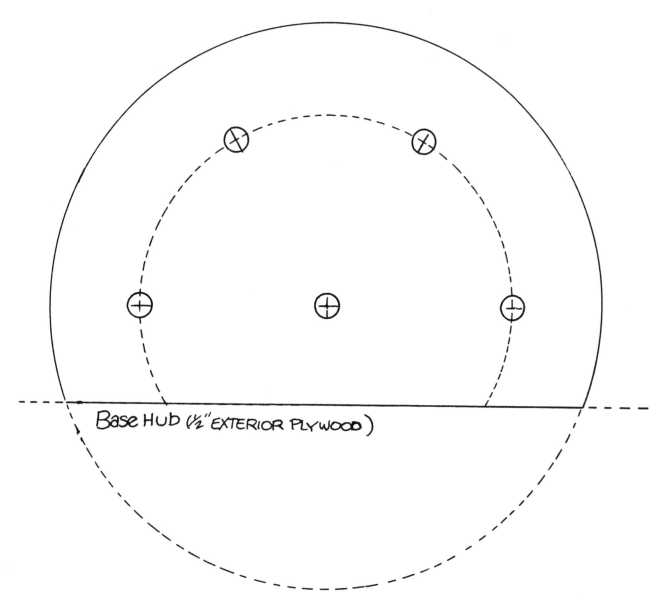

Base Hub (½" EXTERIOR PLYWOOD)

NOTES ON GEODESIC DOME GREENHOUSE CONT.
IF WE MAKE A ¼" ERROR ON ONE STRUT
(STRUTS ARE THE MEMBERS THAT CON-
NECT TO HUBS, HUBS ARE THE THINGS THAT
CONNECT THE STRUTS TOGETHER) WE
CAN PROBABLY STILL CONNECT THE
STRUT TO ITS CORRESPONDING HUB,
BUT EVENTUALLY WE FIND THAT THE
PROBLEM HAS ACTUALLY ONLY BEEN
TRANSFERRED TO ANOTHER PART OF
THE STRUCTURE. LENGTHENING OR
SHORTENING THE STRUT AT THAT
POINT WILL CAUSE SOMETHING TO BE
WRONG AT ANOTHER POINT, AD INFINITUM.
SO DO IT RIGHT THE FIRST TIME.
ACTUALLY THIS PARTICULAR DESIGN IS
MUCH MORE FORGIVING THAN MOST
OTHERS, SO WITH REASONABLE CARE
YOU SHOULDN'T HAVE TOO MANY PROB-
LEMS WITH THE STRUCTURE

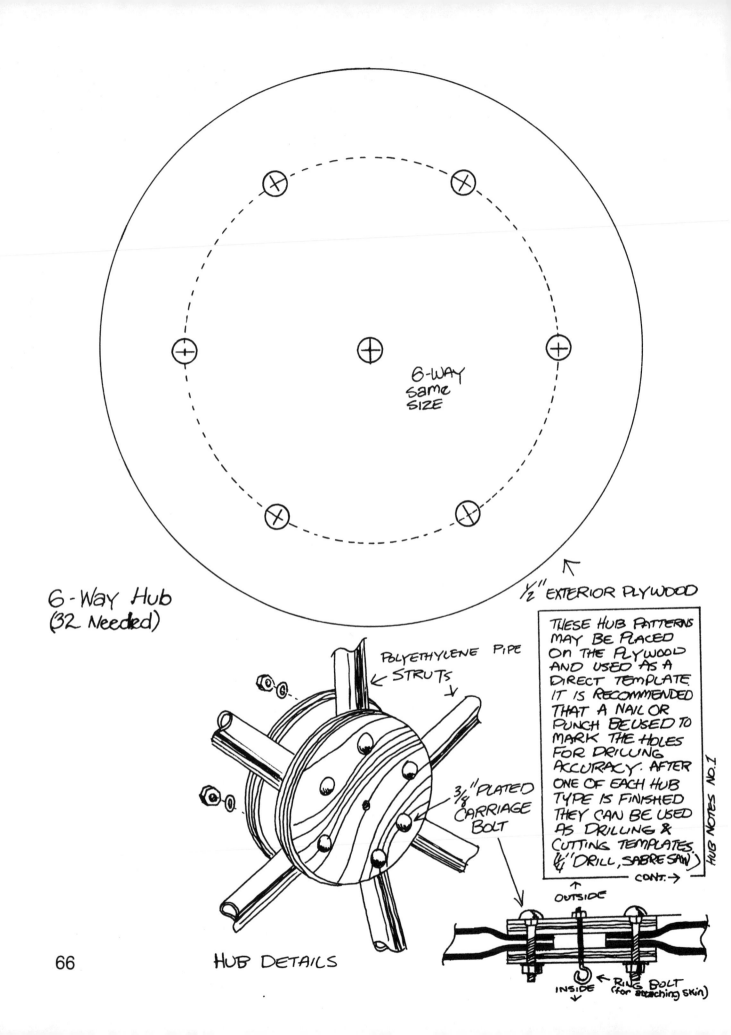

6-Way Hub
(32 Needed)

6-WAY
same
SIZE

½" EXTERIOR PLYWOOD

POLYETHYLENE PIPE
STRUTS

3/8" PLATED
CARRIAGE
BOLT

THESE HUB PATTERNS
MAY BE PLACED
ON THE PLYWOOD
AND USED AS A
DIRECT TEMPLATE.
IT IS RECOMMENDED
THAT A NAIL OR
PUNCH BE USED TO
MARK THE HOLES
FOR DRILLING
ACCURACY. AFTER
ONE OF EACH HUB
TYPE IS FINISHED
THEY CAN BE USED
AS DRILLING &
CUTTING TEMPLATES.
(¼" DRILL, SABRE SAW)

CONT. →

HUB NOTES NO.1

OUTSIDE

INSIDE

RING BOLT
(for attaching skin)

66

HUB DETAILS

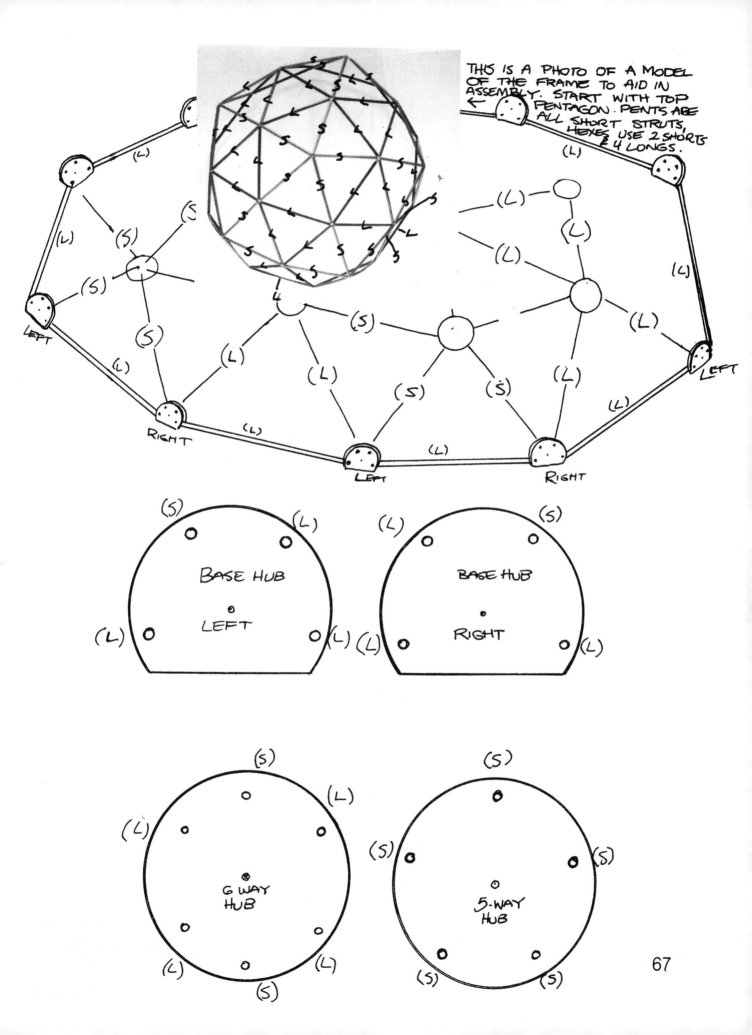

THIS IS A PHOTO OF A MODEL OF THE FRAME TO AID IN ASSEMBLY. START WITH TOP PENTAGON. PENTS ARE ALL SHORT STRUTS, HEXES USE 2 SHORTS & 4 LONGS.

BASE HUB LEFT

BASE HUB RIGHT

6 WAY HUB

5-WAY HUB

67

Option for simpler door

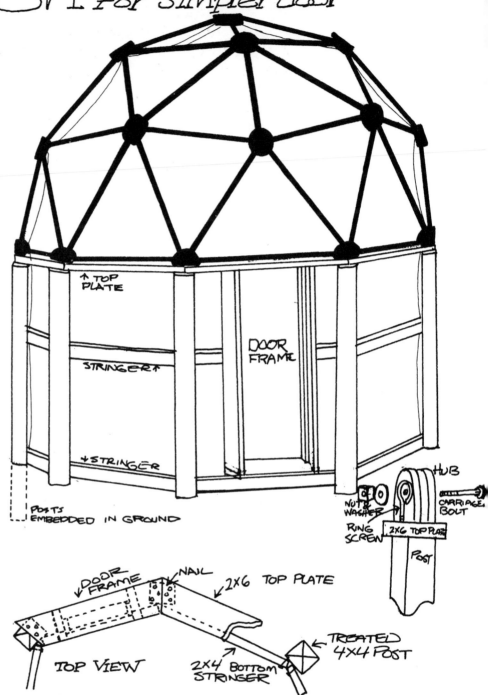

↑ TOP PLATE

DOOR FRAME

STRINGER↑

↓STRINGER

POSTS EMBEDDED IN GROUND

HUB

NUT & WASHER

RING SCREW

CARRIAGE BOLT

2x6 TOP PLATE

POST

↓DOOR FRAME

NAIL

↙2x6 TOP PLATE

TOP VIEW

2x4 BOTTOM STRINGER

↙TREATED 4x4 POST

USING ASSEMBLED DOME AS REFERENCE, DIG POST HOLES AND SINK POSTS, 1 PER HUB. ADD EXTENSION TO SKIN SKIRT. SKIN IS FASTENED TO DOME, THEN DOME IS PLACED ONTO POSTS & MOUNTED (SEE DETAIL). SKIN IS THEN STAPLED TO POSTS & STRINGERS. DOOR FRAME IS CONVENTIONAL. DOOR IS SAME AS WINDOW UNIT #1.

TO MAKE SKIN:

THERE ARE 2 SIZES OF TRIANGLES INVOLVED. AFTER THE FRAME IS ASSEMBLED - DO 2 CARDBOARD TEMPLATES OF EXACT SIZE FOR LAYING OUT SKIN PANELS. ONE TEMPLATE FOR HEX TRIANGLES ONE FOR PENT. TRIANGLES. AFTER INDIVIDUAL PANELS ARE ASSEMBLED, THEY ARE SEALED TOGETHER USING FRAME AS A GUIDE.

OVERLAP & HEAT SEAL

ALLOW FOR OVERLAP

HEXAGON LAYOUT

PENTAGON LAYOUT

THE CONDUIT GREENHOUSE PLAN SHOWS THE METHOD OF ATTACHING SKIN TO FRAME WITH THE MARBLE & CORD METHOD. IT'S DONE EXACTLY THE SAME.

These plans offer you a variety of alternatives. If none of them are exactly what you need, you can adapt those parts that you need for your own design. At the very least, these plans should point out how simple it is to build your own greenhouse. No matter how little experience you have had worked with tools and materials, by following one of these plans, or by adapting it to suit your requirements, you should be able to build a unit you can be proud of.

It should be noted that many homes and apartments have an especially sunny room or alcove, or perhaps an enclosed porch, that prove to be excellent environments for a variety of plants. However, they cannot be considered greenhouses, and they are not discussed in this book. A greenhouse is an enclosure designed to provide protection and a balanced environment for plants — while such an area should be plesant to work in, it is not a room intended for human habitation. Several of the books listed in the bibliography discuss the furnishing of a "plant room" inside the home.

Chapter 10
CLIMATE CONTROL

Your greenhouse is much more than a room for growing plans: it is a compact eco-system. But unlike natural eco-systems, like our planet, it is one that you must set in motion. Your plants do not simply vacation in a greenhouse, basking tourist-like in the abundant light. Sunlight spurs their growth, but it alone cannot sustain them. Growing plants need a steady supply of humidity, water, warmth and fresh air. All of these vital elements must interact, and there must be neither too much nor too little of any of them if your greenhouse is to function properly.

To set the system in motion — and to maintain it — you will need the assistance of some mechanical devices. You will need a heating system, to generate warmth when the nights are cold enough to chill and damage your plants. You will need some means of supplying fresh air regularly, such as one or several vents installed near the roof of your unit. You will need some method of generating humidity, when the air in your unit becomes dry enough to harm the plants. And, you will have to supply your plants with water at least once or twice a week. None of these requirements are difficult to fulfill, and can be provided inexpensively. But **all** these elements must be present or else your plants will fail. They may also fail if there is an imbalance among the elements.

Each of these requirements must be present in the correct proportion to all the others. The more sunlight, the more humidity and water must be provided. Conversely, the less light, the less humidity and water should be provided. And when you are heating the greenhouse in chilly weather you must continue to generate humidity in sufficient quantities to make certain that the air does not become dangerously dry. Fresh air must be supplied at regular intervals every day of the year, in order to keep the air in the unit from becoming either overheated or stagnant.

In a greenhouse, **you** must assume many of the functions of nature. That is not, however, nearly as difficult or costly as it may sound. Many heating and humidity systems are automatic, as are many ventilating systems. Controlled by thermostats that you set, these systems automatically turn on and off as they are required. And these systems are modestly priced. You can establish your "eco-system" for a modest cost, and maintain it with a minimal amount of effort.

Some greenhouse gardeners prefer to automate their units as much as possible. I don't agree — to me, the point of having a greenhouse is to **work** in it, to be intimately involved in all the processes of plant life. I really don't need a machine to do what I enjoy doing. I do, however, agree that a heater, a ventilating system and a humidifier are necessary mechanisms that add, rather than distract from enjoying my greenhouse.

You can do as much — and within bounds, as little — as you like with "machines" in your greenhouse. What you do, after you secure the basics, depends on how you view your unit, the time you have to tend to it, and the amount of money you can afford to spend.

As with all other aspects of greenhouse gardening, your imagination is the most important tool you have. You may be able to come up with a better, or less expensive method for heating your unit or generating humidity. You can certainly try.

There are no mysteries concerning these requirements of light and water and air. This chapter discusses the basic rules for estimating what your plants need, as well as compared the types of mechanisms available to satisfy each of these needs. And once you have selected and installed the basics, you can turn your full attention to the reason for building your greenhouse — to raise plants.

HUMIDITY

Warm air that does not contain a substantial amount of humidity will rapidly wither, and even kill many of the plants in your greenhouse.

Humidity is water suspended in the air as a vapor. The familiar phrase "relative humidity" refers to the percentage of moisture in the air at a given time and location, as measured against the total amount of moisture that air could hold without the moisture being precipitated into rain or fog. For instance, a reading of 50% humidity would indicate that the air at present contains half of the moisture it could hold, without that moisture condensing and becoming visible as droplets.

Most plants require air rich with humidity. The warmer the climate, the more humidity they need. And when they don't get it, their leaves will brown, yellow or drop off. Flower buds will shrivel and fail to open. Plants become especially vulnerable to pest or disease attacks when they are in a weakened state due to the lack of humidity.

Plants normally draw water up from their roots to aid in the many processes of growth. Some of the water is "transpired" — that is, given off as a vapor from the plants pores. Because heat without humidity will dry plants out, the warmer it gets, the more plants will transpire in an attempt to raise the humidity in the atmosphere. But a plant's supply of water is limited, and once it is exhausted the plant will be left parched, lacking the moisture for other necessary operations and in a damagingly dry environment.

In a rain forest, as well as in many other natural environments, the air is generally quite humid. But in a greenhouse, the natural processes responsible for that humidity have been eliminated. You have assumed responsibility for the climate, and so you must generate additional humidity as long as your plants are growing. When plants become dormant, all of their needs — including the need for a large supply of humidity — are substantially decreased.

Most plants do well in an atmosphere averaging 50% to 70% relative humidity. Several methods can be used to maintain such a level in your greenhouse. If you have a small greenhouse, you can rely on a garden hose and your watering can. Make certain that you simply water down the floor and under the benches of your unit several times a day. Purchase a nozzle for the hose that will convert the stream of water into a fine spray mist. In addition to the hose, use your watering can to direct a fine spray onto the plants. While this method should suffice, on very warm days you may exhaust yourself running in and out of the unit like some comical fireman, dragging your hose behind you.

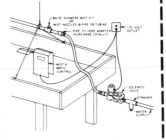

Misting Systems

A Mist System in a greenhouse can be used for three different purposes: Propagating cuttings. . . . Controlling humidity. . . . Evaporative cooling in Summer.

For a system of your own design, we can supply individual mist nozzles, time clocks, humidistats, and solenoid valves. For a basic installation, a simple Mist Propagation Kit which comes ready to assemble and connect to your water supply is available. For fully automatic control, we offer a sophisticated Mist-a-matic unit which controls misting according to the actual watering needs of your plants.

Humidification

Should you plan to cultivate plants, like orchids, which require extra humidity, you'll want to consider a good Humidifier. Our humidifiers, which are made for us by specialists, are efficient and moderately priced. A number of different models are available. The type of unit you select will depend on the size and humidity requirements of your greenhouse. As with all L & B equipment, our representative stands ready to help you with authoritative and experienced suggestions.

Or, you can purchase a humidifier. A humidifier is a compact unit that manufactures humidity from a supply of water (many humidifiers can be hooked up to a garden hose). A humidistat control, much like the control box of a heating system, can be connected to the humidifier. You can set the control for a humidity level of from 15% to 75%, and the control will automatically activate your humidifier when the pre-established level falls too low. Humidifiers adequate for a greenhouse up to 10' long cost as little as $30. In addition, humidistat control units cost from $10 to $15. Both items are available from many greenhouse manufacturers and suppliers.

In my opinion, the installation of a humidifying system will soon pay back the cost of installation, in shiny, healthy plants, and in the labor it saves you. Although I am not an advocate of the automated greenhouse, there are some automatic systems that I consider well worth having — and a humidifying system would certainly be near the top of the list.

Whatever method you adopt in dealing with humidity, you should have a hygrometer. A hygrometer is a small, portable instrument that measures the amount of humidity in the air. There are a number of versions of the hygrometer available, and many cost less than $10. I consider this instrument a necessity, whether you use it by itself or as a double-check on your humidifying system. You can stand or hang it anywhere in your greenhouse, or move it about to take comparative readings. Buy one, and consult it daily. On very warm summer days, check it several times.

Excessive humidity is a much rarer problem in a greenhouse. Only when you have been generating too much humidity, or when temperatures outside fall quite rapidly, will you be confronted with the necessity of lowering the level of humidity. Too much humidity, if sustained over a length of time, can encourage rots on plant tissue. Your hygrometer will tell you when you have a dangerously high level, if you do not personally sense the change in the atmosphere. Any reading over 70%, if it shows no signs of decreasing, is too high for most plants. You can dissipate the moisture by opening the vents in the end wall (or walls) of your unit. Or you can turn the heat on, **briefly**. If you run the heat too long, you'll find your relative humidity has plummeted dangerously low. Watch the hygrometer closely until the moisture level has stabilized around the 50%-60% mark.

As with all other aspects of greenhouse gardening, you must know the needs of your plants. Different types of plants require different levels of humidity. Desert plants, such as cacti, require a low relative humidity. Exotic or tropical plants need a large amount of humidity. Fortunately, most plants do very well in the middle range. Of course, you can always alter the amount of humidity, depending on your observations of the reactions of your plants. And remember — while there must always be some humidity in the air, that amount must be adjusted according to the season and time of day. During the summer you must have some sort of system for regularly supplying humidity. During winter and late fall days, and throughout the year at night, the amount of humidity the plants need will be much lower.

VENTILATION

Your greenhouse should have some mechanism, either automatic or hand-operated, to allow you to admit and regulate a supply of fresh air. Your greenhouse is designed to admit a maximum amount of sunlight, and on a sunny day the temperature in your unit will climb rapidly. If fresh air is not periodically admitted, the air in the unit can become overheated, and its moisture content will entirely evaporate.

Warm dry air can prove harmful to your plants. In addition, the increasingly hot air will move towards the roof of the unit, while cooler air will sink towards the floor, causing temperature flactuations and pockets of varying temperatures — both harmful to your plants. Fresh air, however, will lower the temperature, and its moisture content will be beneficial to the plants. The regular admittance of fresh air will set in motion currents of air that will circulate over and around the plants — something the plants seem to appreciate, as long as they are not in a direct draft.

The most common form of greenhouse ventilation is the use of vents located at the peaks of the end walls or along the upper portion of the roof, on either side of the unit. The idea is that because hot air rises, the vents will have their greatest effect located where they can carry off the overheated air and gradually introduce cooler, fresh ait that will filter down into the unit. As they are located well above the majority of plants in a unit, the chance of a damagingly cool draft blowing directly across the plants is greatly reduced.

These vents, sometimes referred to as roof sashes, can be operated manually by push rods or gears, or automatically, which calls for a more elaborate system, which may include a thermostat and a motor to adjust the vents. Many automatic systems also feature the use of an exhaust fan. When the temperature rises too much, the thermostat starts the fan, which draws out the warm air, while a vent on the opposite end wall of the unit is opened to allow cool air to enter.

The ventilation system you need is largely determined by convenience and cost. Any of the above mentioned systems will do the job. Two manual vents would certainly be the least expensive method, and they would do the job. A fan and vent system makes an excellent ventilating system. Run by a thermostat, it has the adventage of working whether or not you are there. Otherwise, if there is no one home on warm summer days, you will have to adjust manual vents in the morning and take your chances. A fan and vent, connected to a pre-set thermostat, eliminates that potential problem. Unless you have a very large greenhouse, and an inflation-proof bank account, I don't recommend an elaborate automated system. Certainly it's very nice, but you just don't need those motors and auto-controlled vents.

Vents alone usually cost between $8 and $10. A fan and vent system, including a

thermostat control, can be purchased for slightly less than $50. Fully automated systems begin at $75, and can cost as much as $175. Many greenhouse manufacturers and companies marketing greenhouse accessories offer a variety of ventilating systems. You must have some means of insuring proper ventilation for your plants. Fortunately, you have a variety of choices, some of them quite low in cost.

LIGHT AND SHADE

Sufficient light is a basic necessity of plant life. Light is the primary ingredient in the process of photosynthesis by which plants manufacture their food. Without enough light, plants weaken, drop their leaves and produce fewer, and frailer, flowers. If a plant is deprived of its required amount of light, it will eventually die.

Insufficient light is rarely a problem in a well-placed greenhouse. However, some greenhouse gardeners have found it useful to supplement the pale, diffuse light of winter with artificial lights. This is not a necessity — even on cloudy days, when we suspect that the plants are receiving no light, some sunlight is reaching them. However, you might find the addition of one fluorescent light, to a selected group of plants, an interesting wintertime experiment.

A much more important problem than increasing the light level for your plants is, ironically, protecting your plants from too **much** light. The long summer days of intense light can prove too much for all but your heartiest cacti and succulents, so you must take action to decrease the amount and strength of the light falling on your plants. Too much light causes wilting, leaf loss and even burns; it also wrings the air dry of all moisture, causing further harm to your plants. The more light, the more heat there is, and the higher the temperature in the unit, the more humidity the plants need to keep from drying out. If the humidity level does not keep pace with the temperature, the plants will draw additional water from their roots to their leaf surfaces, in an attempt to keep cool. But if the situation is not alleviated, the plants will soon run out of water, and some of their exposed parts may be burned, while the entire plant will noticeably wilt and sag.

What can you do?

Your ventilation system will pay back your investment at a time like this. As soon as the temperature reaches a pre-set point on the thermostat, the exhaust fan will automatically turn itself on, and the vent will open to admit fresh, and somewhat cooler air. If you have an entirely manual ventilation system, you will have to adjust the vents and watch your greenhouse thermometer to determine when the danger is over.

But a ventilation system cannot solve the problem alone. It can lower the unit's temperature, but it cannot screen the plants from the momentarily damaging rays of the sun. You will have to do that yourself, using one of several methods. You can attach aluminum, wood or vinyl shades to the greenhouse, draping them over the glass or plastic surface. Or you can apply a paste shading compound directly to the glass surface.

The panels of aluminum are composed of slats fastened to a wooden or aluminum frame.

The wooden shades resemble large window blinds, as they are composed of wooden slats, and extended or retracted by a system of ropes and pulleys rather like the controls used on window shades. The slats are often coated with aluminum paint. The vinyl plastic shades are made of a semi-transparent, tough but flexible vinyl film which is said to reduce the light falling upon the plants by as much as 65%. Unlike the other shades, it is applied to the **inside** surface of the glass. You must first cut the plastic to the appropriate length and width. Then you must wash down the glass thoroughly — but don't allow it to dry.

Immediately press the plastic against the glass with long sweeps of your palm, a stiff brush or a squeegee. The tension established between the water on the glass and the plastic will hold the sheet in place. The plastic can be easily removed and reused many times. It cannot, however, be effectively applied to any other surface but glass and give the same results.

There are shading powders available, which must be dissolved in water and sprayed onto the glass. You must be careful to apply an even coat everywhere, so that there are no great variations, causing too much, or too little light to penetrate different parts of the unit.

Greenhouse Shading

There will be times when you'll need some type of shading to reduce heat and light in your greenhouse, usually from late Spring to early Fall. The amount of shading and time of application will depend upon where you live and what you grow.

Aluminum Roll-up Shades

The roll-up type is most practical and easily adjusted from the outside as weather and sunlight vary. These quality Aluminum Shades are factory-assembled, ready for installation. They are light-weight, roll up and down neatly, and are made of long-life, maintenance-free extruded aluminum. They reduce the incoming light by about 70%.

Vinyl Plastic Film Shades

An attractive green, are inexpensive and easy to install. You cut each panel to the proper size. Wash down the inside of the glass with a sponge or hose, then smooth the plastic onto the wet glass with a stiff wallpaper brush or squeegee. Just peel off when not needed, and reuse next season. Reduces light by about 65%.

Many greenhouse manufacturers offer a wide selection of shades. Some are designed to be used with their own units, while others can be used on any greenhouse. Incidentally, the most recent development in shades is the introduction of fiberglass shading panels, so you might investigate this material.

When should you shade your unit? Only when you must, I believe. Some gardeners apply shading and leave it on for a length of time. I prefer shades that can be quickly applied and removed, allowing me to shade the unit, or a part of the unit, **only** when I judge it to be necessary. Shading is necessary on bright summer days, but it isn't necessary on dim summer days, when it may serve to further decrease the amount of light available to your plants. That may not be a serious problem, but I don't see any reason to take unnecessary chances.

But **when** should you shade? You can determine that by observing your plants. If the foliage on a number of plants yellows of wilts, or if leaves develop brown spots, and you can discover no other causes for these symptoms, put up the shading. Your greenhouse is supposed to maximize growing conditions, including sunlight, so don't shade unless your plants show signs of being in trouble. Morning sunlight is not generally strong enough to be damaging. Late morning and early afternoon, however, comprise the most potentially harmful period during the summer. If you must leave your greenhouse unattended during the day, you will have to make an educated guess in the morning, using the weather report to guide you. And if your guess is wrong one day, and you did not put the shades on when they were needed, don't be too worried. With prompt care, most of your plants should rapidly recover from their sunburn.

Don't shade first and ask questions later. Use shade when you must, and only when you must. Too much shade, like too much light, is never a good idea.

You will probably require a supply of electricity for your unit, to run an electric heater or drive an exhaust fan. If you have experience with installing electric wiring, you can do the job jourself. Or you can have a licensed electrician do the job. I suggest that you have several outlets installed in the unit at the same time, including at least one socket to provide overhead illumination. Just one or two 100 watt bulbs can extend the number of hours you can spend working in your unit. And if the evenings are the only time you have to work in your greenhouse, you certainly must have adequate illumination.

While you may not immediately need outlets, you may find that at some point you will want to use an electric tool or appliance to simplify your gardening. And having an outlet in the unit is a good deal simpler than running an extension cord from your home. Make certain that all of the wiring is done with moisture-proof materials.

Artificial light can be used in a greenhouse to supplement dull winter light, or to increase your growing area. In addition, if you have been compelled by a lack of space to locate your greenhouse on the north side of your property, artificial light can help you grow a number of flowering plants that normally require several hours of bright light daily.

You can purchase fluorescent tubes — new or used — and fittings and install them in your unit, or you can buy a pre-assembled lighting unit designed to be used with plants. Two to three 40 watt fluorescent tubes must be used for each two by four foot area of growing space. To supplement winter light, you should keep the tubes on for four to six hours daily. If you turn them on in the late afternoon and run them into the evening, you can bring some annual plants into early bloom, by convincing them that spring has arrived.

You can extend your growing space by installing a fluorescent tube under a **watertight** bench, and cultivating plants that require bright light. Or, you can brighten a dark corner with artificial light.

But you must use moisture-proof fittings and materials.

If you are considering the use of artificial light, remember that you will have some small additional monthly increase in your operating costs. However, fluorescent tubes are well suited for use in a greenhouse, as they are most economical when they are on for a lengthy period of time.

WATER

Providing sufficient water for your plants is one of the most important functions in a greenhouse. You can either manually water the plants, or install a watering system, but whatever method is chosen you must supply water in sufficient quantities on a regular basis if your plants are to survive and prosper.

Plants absorb water from the soil by means of their roots. Water is drawn in through the roots and is then transported to all parts of a plant. Water is the medium that carries nutrients throughout a plant, and is thus a vital component in a plant's production of food. Excess water is given off (transpired) as vapor from a plant's leaf surfaces.

The simplest and most inexpensive method of watering plants is to use a long spouted watering can, and to water each plant from above in succession. Poke the spout down into the foliage, and apply water to the soil, **not** the foliage. Plants don't need large droplets of water on their leaves — they need water in the soil, where they can absorb it as they need it.

If you have a small greenhouse or if, like many of us, you are gardening under the budget, I suggest you stick to watering by hand. Watering all of the plants two to three times every week should not take up an inordinate amount of time, and it allows you an opportunity to take a close look at each of your plants.

A variety of ingenious automatic watering systems have been devised, and if you dislike watering by hand or if you have a very large greenhouse, you might want to consider automating the watering.

Wick watering seems to be one of the most popular of the systems. Separate wicks connect each plant with a resevoir of water established an inch or two below the plants. Water is drawn up through the wick and into the plant's soil by capillary action, and as long as the resevoir is kept filled the soil of the plants will be moist. A wick is connected to a pot by drawing it through the pot's drainage hole. The end of the wick is flattened along the bottom of the pot, and a layer of fine soil is placed over it. Above this layer the normal potting soil is added. The fine soil poses little resistance to the upward motion of the water.

If you are potting plants directly into the benches, there is a system available that offers a flexible plastic hose with spray nozzles that can be attached along the perimeter of the bench. Such a system can be controlled automatically, by means of a clock that adjusts valves to regulate both the frequency and length of the watering. A rather similar system offers a length of plastic hose preforated with many tiny holes, which is laid on the soil surface of a bench. The hose must be attached to a faucet, and when you intend to water you need only turn on the faucet, forcing water through the hose and out of the tiny apertures.

Many greenhouse manufacturers carry a variety of automatic and semi-automatic watering systems. While they save you some time and effort, many of the systems are expensive and all of them would necessitate the installation of plumbing. If you can devote only so much money to building and stocking your unit, and no more, I believe that you can get along handily without such a system. Indeed, many gardeners find watering a pleasant task that they prefer to do themselves.

Plant Watering Systems

Whether you grow directly in soil-filled benches, or in separate pots, flats, or containers, you can do a better job of watering with one of L & B's labor-saving Plant Watering Systems.

These systems are covered in detail in our Equipment and Accessory catalog. Your local L & B representative will be glad to arrange for your copy.

Even if you don't install a watering system, you may want to run water into the greenhouse to simplify your watering chores. Having to fetch and carry water into the unit could turn a pleasant activity into a time-consuming task. However, the cost of running a pipe into the unit, if the unit is any distance from your home, would be substantial — unless you did the job yourself. While running water, in the form of a tub and faucet, would be a positive addition to your unit, you can adapt to conditions and get along without it. It is only really necessary when you have a very large unit, requiring a volume of water for everyday tasks. In fact, a tub might take up too much room in a small greenhouse — room that could otherwise be used for growing plants.

If you have an outdoor faucet close at hand, you can attach a hose to the faucet and bring the hose into your greenhouse. One ingenious idea I have heard of in use suggests placing a large tub or a small barrel in your unit. The container is filled with water and positioned directly in front of your heater. When the heater is on, the warm air blowing across the container will cause moisture to evaporate, thus increasing the level of humidity in the unit. The tub can double as a ready supply of water for use in the unit, as long as it is kept fresh and remains clean and free of scum.

You must water your plants, and you must water them on a regular basis. But you needn't spend much money doing it. Although watering your plants is one of the most important functions you have in a greenhouse, it is also one of the least expensive.

HEAT

You will have to heat your greenhouse. Even if you live in an area having the mildest of winters, there will still be occasional frosts — and even one night of frost can prove lethal to some of your plants. How much heat you will have to provide depends on the severity of your climate, the size of your greenhouse and the kinds of plants you are growing.

Some gardeners simply extend their home heating systems to their units. While this would seem to be the most inexpensive method of heating a greenhouse, it does present some difficulties. Your plants and your family may have differing temperature requirements — a situation that can only lead to trouble for your plants. You will be supplying heat for your unit — but will you be supplying sufficient warmth, at those times when your unit needs it?

Installing a heater in your greenhouse need not be a difficult or expensive procedure. Many heaters are quite compact. Some are also relatively inexpensive to purchase and operate. And, because they are located in your unit, they can respond to temperature fluctuations there and only there, turning on and off as the plants require warmth.

Gas, oil and electric greenhouse heaters are available from many greenhouse manufacturers. One of the factors influencing your selection of a heater should be the cost of utilities in your area. Try to match your heater with the least expensive utility. However, it is also worth keeping in mind that electric heaters are the least expensive heaters, costing from $50 to $150. They can be installed easily and quickly. And they are also generally the smallest heaters, making them especially good for use in a greenhouse where every inch of space counts. Gas and oil units tend to take up more room and to require a larger outlay of funds to purchase and install. If you live in an area having very mild winters, you certainly need no more than a small electric heater to protect your plants through those occasional frosts.

No-Vent Gas Heater

The No-Vent takes little space inside the greenhouse. Its combustion chamber is outside the greenhouse entirely sealed-off. It consumes no greenhouse air and it requires no chimney. Built-in blower fans provide even, draft-free, heat distribution. Furnished for either LP or natural gas, it's one of the most popular greenhouse unit heaters.

Be certain that the heater you are considering includes a thermostat. For the thermostat can be pre-set to a temperature, and when the temperature falls below that setting on the thermostat, the heater will be turned on automatically. When the temperature climbs high enough, the heater will turn itself off.

While you will certainly need some sort of heater, it is well worth the effort to reduce the frequency with which it must be used. For instance, each fall you should check

your unit for any apertures admitting drafts. Use watherstripping or putty to seal them. Because many of the coldest of winter winds seem to blow from the north, you might consider insulating the northern wall of your unit with themopane to reduce the amount of cold leaking into your unit. If your utility bills are simply getting too large to carry, you can always change the kinds of plants you grow. Foliage plants, and some flowering plants, do quite well in temperatures of 55° to 60°. Only grow the kinds of plants you can afford to grow. Don't plan on a large crop of tropical plants if you cannot afford the large utility bills that are sure to result.

While you must heat your unit if you are to use it at all through the late fall and winter months, you can do so at moderate expense if you shop carefully for the heater you need, if you do everything you can to weatherproof your unit, and if you decide beforehand on what kinds of plants you intend to grow. Remember — your greenhouse is supposed to be a pleasurable activity, not an economic liability.

Soil heating cables are insulated coils designed to be placed beneath the soil in a bench. They supply an even, constant warmth to mature plants, cuttings or seedlings. While coils cannot replace a heater, they can prove a valuable supplement to it, if your plants are growing in benches, and not in pots. Coils can also be used to transform a coldframe into a hotbed.

Electric Heaters

The perfect answer for heating a small greenhouse, or adding supplemental heat to an existing system. Easy to install, they are completely automatic with built-in thermostat and powerful air-circulation fan. These heaters may be attached to a vertical surface, mounted overhead, or installed under a bench.

Chapter 11
FURNISHINGS

In any greenhouse, you need a space reserved for working with individual plants, where you can pot a plant, transplant it, take a cutting or treat it for an insect infestation or an infection. Your work area should be at least 2' by 3'. Use a piece of plywood or some other wood to make a bench for the working surface. The best place to establish the area is in a corner, where you can attach the sheet to the walls of your unit, and further support it with wooden legs.

Use the space beneath the bench to store your soil components in their original bags or in sealed, carefully labeled containers. You can also store your fertilizer and any containers of chemicals under the bench, along with any large gardening tools. You might consider hanging a painted pegboard on one wall, so that you will have a convenient place to neatly store your tools where you can see and easily reach them. Stock extra pots under the bench, according to their size. On the flat work surface you might want to keep some small tools immediately at hand, as well as a pencil and notebook. Perhaps you might even have a space for books on greenhouse gardening, so that you can consult them immediately as needed.

Remember, however, that your greenhouse probably has more heat and humidity then any tool shed or library shelf. Tools left exposed and unprotected may quickly rust, and books can become damp and fall apart, unless you anticipate these problems beforehand. Make certain that your tools are coated against rust; if they are not, you can always paint them with a rustproofing enamel or paint. Keep your books away from watering areas — better yet, wrap them in plastic bags to protect them. In this way you won't lose any tools or books though neglect.

I know of one gardener who suspended a small shelf along one side of his working area, and divided the shelf into slots. He kept his seeds, labeled and carefully separated, there along with other small and easily lost items.

Yes, I know it does subtract from your growing area. But you **need** a working area, reserved for preparing soil and chemical mixes and for working on individual plants.

You need it, and you need to keep it clean. When you're through working on it, clean it off. Discard excess soil spilled on the surface, as well as any foliage that you have removed from the plant. If you have been working with chemicals, wash the area thoroughly when you are finished.

Some gardeners install a tub next to their working area, complete with hot and cold running water. Such an arrangement certainly makes many procedures easier and faster — but it can be quite expensive. The tub, complete with faucets, can be purchased from a number of sources, such as a plumbing supply company or from several greenhouse manufacturers. It is not that expensive. But the cost of hiring a plumber to extend a water pipe from your house and hook it up to the sink can be very costly. While having a sink would save you time and effort or carrying in water as you need it, it is not really a necessity. You can get along without it, at least at first. Indeed, if you have a relatively small greenhouse, you may simply not have the room to contain it. But no matter how small your unit is, anything larger than a window greenhouse should have a work area, doubling as a storage space for greenhouse utensils and supplies.

SOIL

Whether you grow plants in benches or pots (or both), you will be growing them in soil. Plants, with some exceptions, will not live without it. Soil has two essential functions: it anchors and supports plants, and it stores the minerals and water necessary for plant growth.

I know that many gardeners spade up soil from their outdoor gardens and use it in their greenhouses. But I do not recommend such a procedure. You may have rows of bright, seemingly healthy plants in your outdoor garden. And you could reason that, if soil is so important to plant growth, this must be awfully good soil you have. And if the soil has had such good results outside, wouldn't it do just as well in your greenhouse?

I don't think so.

Certainly the soil you dig up may have a

number of nutrients. But it will also assuredly have insect eggs, insect larvae, fungus infections, bacteria, animal droppings and other harmful effluvia. All of them are trouble, and some are certainly fatal to indoor plants.

Yes, those plants outdoors seem to be doing well. They are probably hardier than many of your greenhouse plants. And their soil is altered by the action of the elements, thus dissipating dangerous concentrations of infectious stuff. A plant in a pot has soil that is not altered. And a greenhouse offers optimum conditions of heat, light and water: such conditions encourage plant growth, but they may also encourage the proliferation of infections.

Greenhouse gardeners have been using garden soil, without substantially treating it for infections, for many years, and evidently without major troubles. But you may prove an exception to that good fortune. My suggestion is to buy your soil components, and mix a potting medium yourself. Or, if you cannot afford to to that, I urge you to at least sterlilize soil before you bring it into the greenhouse.

Soil is not a singular material. Rather, it is a remarkably rich collection of organic and non-organic substances. Organic materials are those originating in living things, such as plants or animals, and through the processes of decay and decomposition they are broken down into elementary substances. Non-organic materials, such as rocks, are reduced by erosion to small shards of material rich in minerals. Each kind of material brings nutrients important to green life into the soil. Water dissolves these particles, thus making the nutrients available to plants.

The soil in your garden might not only be harboring infections — it might also **not** have the best balance of nutrients and consistency for plants. You will find that your plants do their best in soil that has been carefully mixed, rather than haphazardly thrown together through the action of time and the elements.

The soil should be "light," so that repeated waterings do not compact it in a lumpish mass around plant roots. It should, in fact, retain water long enough to benefit a plant, but not so long as to harm it. A soil mix that is too fine will not hold water — liquid will simply run through the soil and out the drainage hole. "Heavy" soil will remain almost constantly wet, depriving a plant of oxygen and thereby creating conditions suitable for a rot or fungus to appear.

But how do you get the soil mix you need?

You can buy it. Commercial soil mixes are available at most garden supply centers. The only drawback to such mixes is the fact that they are costly when you must purchase in quantity. They are marketed primarily for people potting a few house plants. Trying to buy a sufficient quantity for your greenhouse could prove a terrific expense. Fortunately, you don't have to.

You can buy separate soil components in large quantities at a substantially lower price. What are the components of a "good" soil?

First of all, topsoil, which has many nutritive elements and acts to retain water, storing it for the plant.

Peat moss is an organic material that acts to aerate the soil. It also has some nutrients.

Humus is a form of peat moss, having similar qualities. It differs in that it has a higher acidic content.

Perlite is a form of expanded volcanic rock. It is used to provide aeration in the soil mix. It is also slightly alkaline.

Vermiculite is a form of mica that has expanded under high temperatures. It increases the drainage capability of the soil. It also helps by retaining some moisture and nutrients.

Cow manure is rich in trace nutrients. It should never be used unless it has been commercially processed, for "fresh" manure will burn a plant's roots.

Dolomitic limestone contains magnesium, an important nutrient. It is very alkaline, and is used to balance an excessively acidic soil.

These are the basic components of a "good" soil mix. You need not use them all, but you must observe a balance of "loose" and "heavy" elements to provide aeration and good soil consistency.

The more books you consult on gardening, the more soil formulas you are bound to discover. The basic soil formula calls for one part topsoil, one part peat moss or humus, and one part perlite. I suggest that, if you have not had much previous experience with mixing soil, you should begin by using such a formula. As you gain experience, you can begin to experiment with other mixes. Many gardeners seem to have a favorite formula, and you can begin to compare such recipes as you meet other greenhouse gardeners.

Large bags of the various soil components are available at many garden supply centers. When you buy in quantity, the cost of the soil is significantly reduced.

But what can you do if your budget just can't stretch to include any soil? Or perhaps you can afford the components, but there simply isn't any supply center carrying the materials in your area. Must you then rely on the unknown quality and doubtful cleanliness of the soil outside your greenhouse door? No.

You can sterilize the soil yourself. Soil mixes and components sold in supply centers have already been sterilized — that is, cleaned of impurities such as bacteria, fungus or pests. Admittedly, it is a task better left to a factory than an individual, but if you have no alternative, you can do it yourself. The simplest method is to mix 2½ tablespoon of commercial formalin (otherwise known as formaldehyde) to every 1 cup of water you use. Use a sheet of plastic to lay down a 2″ layer of soil. Sprinkle the water treated with formalin as evenly as possible over the soil surface. Don't drench the soil, but apply sufficiently so that the soil everywhere is moist. Then turn and mix the soil thoroughly. Store the treated soil in clean containers, such as boxes or unused propagation flats. I know of one gardener who uses new garbage cans to hold the treated soil. Cover the containers immediately with a sheet of plastic. After 24 hours remove the covering and allow the soil to air. Don't use the soil until all traces of the strong formalin aroma have disappeared. That may take several days. Whenever you are working with formalin, you should be careful not to inhale the fumes, as they are quite powerful. While the soil is airing, move it into a protected space, so that it may not accidentally become reinfected or infested with pests. A large, clean container with a lid makes an excellent permanent storage unit for the soil. You could store the soil in the space under your work area, or in a garage or shed. But wherever you keep it, after it has been thoroughly aired, **keep the lid on**. Migrating insects, or wind blown infections might otherwise end up in what you trusted to be sterilized soil.

Sterilizing soil can be a tiresome, time consuming project — but if this is the only way you can obtain "clean" soil you may find it well worth the effort. Whether or not you decide to use sterilized soil is entirely up to you. Many experienced greenhouse gardeners have used unsterilized soil for years and reported no ill effects to their plants. In my opinion, it is just too much of a risk. There are enough potentially troublesome situations in gardening without adding to existing problems. Ninety-nine times out of one hundred, unsterilized soil may give no problem. But I have always suspected that I would encounter that one occasion when real trouble emerged as a result of using soil spaded out of my garden.

FERTILIZER

Fertilizers, sometimes called plant "foods," are preparations consisting of one or more of the nutrients necessary for healthy plant growth, green foliage and well-formed, colorful flowers. Outdoors, these elements are constantly replenished in the soil by the actions of erosion and decomposition. When you remove a plant, bringing it into an artificial environment, you deprive it of these natural actions, and you must personally assume the responsibility of regularly resupplying these nutrients.

What elements do plants require, and what do they do?

Plants require relatively large amounts of nitrogen, potassium and phosphorus, and lesser amounts of calcium, magnesium, iron, zinc and several others. Basically, all of these elements are fuel to "run" a plant, necessary components of the processes by which a plant produces its own food.

Nitrogen helps stimulate steady plant growth. It also strengthens plant stems and is one of the elements indirectly responsible for the characteristic green color of plant foliage.

Potassium helps a plant resist disease. It is one of the components of the manufacture of plant sugars and starches. Potassium is also important in the development of strong, healthy roots.

Phosphorus is a vital part of the production of "food" (plant sugars) within a plant. It also triggers the mechanism by which energy, released by the sugars being "burned off" within the plant, is distributed to its various parts. Phosphorus encourages strong, disease-resistant roots.

These three elements are absolutely essential for plant health and growth. Calcium, magnesium and sulfur are also important, but they are required in smaller amounts. Calcium influences the growth of plant cells and the root system. Magnesium is an important part of the manufacture of chlorophyll, the substance that gives plants their green color. Chlorophyll is, in turn, a part of the process of photosynthesis, by which a plant generates further energy for growth.

"Trace" elements must be present, but they are needed in very small amounts. Iron, zinc, manganese, boron, molybdenum, copper and chlorine are all trace elements.

What happens when these nutrients are not present?

A lack of nitrogen often leads to stunted growth, thin, weak stems and pale foliage. If a plant is receiving insufficient potassium, its growth rate may gradually slow, until its over-all weakness and blotched leaves identify the problem. Too little phosphorus will cause a plant to shed leaves and begin to wilt. The remaining leaves become quite yellow along their margins. In other words, when a plant is not receiving the raw materials that act as fuel for many of its vital processes, it begins to weaken and break down in a number of ways. Little by little, it ceases to

function, and if the condition is not remedied, it will finally die.

So you must regularly feed your plants. And because you are growing them in a greenhouse, you have to feed them more often than plants kept in other environments. Because they are receiving optimum amounts of light, moisture and warmth they are going to grow, and keep on growing. Growth requires fuel, and if they don't have the raw materials to manufacture the fuel, you're in trouble, and they're in trouble.

How do you "feed" a plant?

Plant "foods" are available as tablets, sticks, powders or liquids. When you're feeding a number of plants, either the powder of the liquid will prove most economical or convenient. It is advisable to establish a feeding schedule, and to adhere to it. If you feed your plants once a week, do so, **every** week — try not to let the schedule lapse. Some gardeners mix a dilute fertilizer into the water that they apply to the plants, thus combining two necessary actions. However, even using a **very** diluted food, they apply it no more than twice a week.

You will find that most fertilizers packages contains instructions and suggested frequencies for feeding.

One of the first things you'll notice about plant food packages is the legend under the brand name, such as 10-15-10 or 15-30-15. The figures refer to the percentages of the three most important nutrients, nitrogen, phosphorus and potassium. Most packages will also indicate what types of plants the food is intended for. A "complete" fertilizer is a fertilizer containing all of these elements, as well as a supply of the other, secondary nutrients.

The type of fertilizer you use is of secondary importance to the frequency of its applications. You may adjust the feeding schedule to your convenience and the needs of your plants, but the most sensible schedule, in my opinion, is a dilute dose of fertilizer given once or twice a week.

HOW PLANTS MAKE THEIR FOOD

Photosynthesis is the process by which plants manufacture their own food. Nutrients are important components of the process, but they are not in themselves plant "food."

Plants manufacture food by collecting energy from the sun, moisture from the soil and carbon dioxide from the air. These raw materials, along with nutrients, become part of a process by which plant sugars are produced for immediate use, or retained as a food supply, or used as one of the basic elements of the plant cells being manufactured.

As the plant sugar is burned, oxygen is drawn into the plant, and carbon dioxide is released — the reverse of the process for gathering a supply of fuel. Photosynthesis, in which food is manufactured, and respiration, when the food is burned up to supply the plants needs, are two complementary processes — or perhaps separate aspects of one process, a marvelous process that is continuous and regenerative. Without photosynthesis, plants couldn't live. Without photosynthesis, life as we know it — including ourselves — couldn't exist on earth, since the ultimate source of all protein comes from plants.

A descriptive listing of the green things that can be grown in a greenhouse would easily be as long as this book — and would undoubtedly still be incomplete. Indeed, you can grow, with varying degrees of difficulty, almost every kind of plant in your greenhouse. I know of one gardener who even begins his trees in his unit, transplanting them when he judges them to be hardy enough to adjust to the outdoors!

Any list of possibilities would have to include all of the many varieties of flowering and foliage plants, as well as bulbs, herbs and vegetables. Out of this multitude of choices, the kinds of plants you select will obviously depend on what attracts your interest or admiration. Not so obviously, your budget should also be considered when you are selecting species for your unit. For some plants require greater care and expense than other varieties. Also, different kinds of plants have very different nighttime temperature requirements. Greenhouses are often referred to as being either "cool", "moderate" or "warm". These terms describe the degree to which they are heated during winter nights. A cool unit is maintained at a temperature of between 45°-50° F. A moderate greenhouse has a nighttime temperature range of 55°-60°. And a warm unit maintains a temperature of at least 65°F. throughout the night. The warmer you must keep your unit, the higher your heating bills. Fortunately, literally hundreds of foliage and flowering plant species do quite well in a cool or moderate greenhouse. Just remember to check on the temperature requirements of a species **before** you decide to grow it. For an excessively warm, or cold, environment can kill a plant faster than most pests and diseases.

This book is primarily concerned with the methods of planning and constructing a greenhouse. While there are few books giving the specifics of building your own unit, there are many books devoted in large part, or entirely, to the selection and care of plants in your greenhouse. Several are listed in the bibliography. After you have selected and built your greenhouse, you will have many years to study plants and become more and more proficient in raising them.

THE pH TEST — ACID AND ALKALINE SOILS

A soil is either acidic or alkaline — you've probably heard that, or read it. But what does that mean, and how does it affect your plants? Anything wet, or capable of being dissolved in water, has some potential for absorbing and retaining the element hydrogen. The greater the potential of a substance for accepting and retaining hydrogen, the more alkaline it becomes.

The pH scale describes the amount of hydrogen a substance can hold. The median of the readings is 7.0, on a scale ranging from 0 to 14. A soil test kit, costing less than $10, will allow you to determine the pH of your soil. It is not a difficult procedure. A pH reading above 7 indicates an alkaline soil, and anything below 7 means that the soil is more acid than alkaline.

Most plants do not do well in a soil having a reading close to 7 — but they can adapt to soils having a reading several points on either side of the median. But if the soil is **too** acidic, or too alkaline, the plants will do poorly. Growth may slow noticeably, leaves will wilt, become discolored and drop off, and the plant may lose its flowers.

Your soil test kit will include instructions for determining the pH level, and suggestions for remedying any potentially harmful imbalance. Although there is no hard and fast rule, there **is** a rough rule of thumb that suggest that most plants prefer a slightly acidic soil (6 to 6.5).

Peat moss, humus or topsoil can be added to a soil mix to increase acidity. Limestone, perlite or eggshells are all very alkaline substances. The idea in preparing a mix is to not rely heavily on any of these substances, but to use portions of each.

Don't fret if your soil tests out at something other than 6.5. Plants can adapt to other pH levels, while some **prefer** other levels. Don't begin juggling a soil mix unless a reading is widely off the median, or your plants are showing signs of real trouble.

GARDENING TOOLS

You need have only a few tools and furnishings to begin gardening in your greenhouse. Indeed, I think you will get off to a much better start by beginning small and working your way up. Get the essential gardening tools, and a small number of hardy plants. Work with them until you have mastered the techniques of plant care. Establish a daily routine, and get yourself into the habit of following it. Take cuttings and try your skill at propagating new plants. Meanwhile, you should be getting the "feel" of your unit — learning how to operate its systems efficiently, without waste. As your confidence and knowledge increase, begin adding to and diversifying your plant collection. You'll probably be amazed at how rapidly that seemingly huge unit has become filled with a wide and colorful variety of green life.

The more you learn about plants, and about the operation of your greenhouse, the more readily you will be able to identify the tools and other materials you now need, the plants or processes you have the most interest in, and the most profitable or efficient manner of running your unit. I have heard of several well-to-do neophyte gardeners who spent lavishly to equip their units, only to discover that some of the items they had bought they did not need, and much of the rest they did not know how to use.

What are the basics? The tools you will certainly need to begin greenhouse gardening include a hand trowel, for turning soil; a sharp knife or a pair of shears for pruning and taking cuttings; gloves; a supply of small wooden stakes for propping up plants or plant parts; a plastic spray bottle for applying a mist of water or for spraying chemicals; and of course, a long-spouted watering can. A can with a long spout will enable you to reach plants on high shelves or in hanging baskets, without risking accidentally dousing plants below. The can should have a capacity of one to two gallons — any larger, and it will prove unwieldy when filled.

That's what you need to begin. As your experience in gardening grows, you will no doubt discover that you need other tools. Knowing what you need, you should have no trouble finding it in a hardware store or a gardening supply center. When you know what you need, get it. But **don't** tie up money that could be used in a number of other ways by investing in tools you don't know how to use, or don't yet need. I think you will find that you never lack for necessary, even vital, expenses in a greenhouse.

What sort of furnishings must you have? Well, you will need a bench, or benches, to hold your plants or your potted plants. You will need pots. You will need soil to fill the benches, or to fill the pots standing on the benches. And you will need fertilizer, to apply to the soil.

Benches are certainly one of the most important items in your greenhouse. They are waist high structures resembling tables, and they are used in one of two ways. Most benches have low walls, and they can be filled with a potting mix, into which plants are rooted. Or, potted plants can be grouped on the benches.

Planting Benches

Planting Benches are a **must** for any greenhouse. Plants are brought up to a convenient growing and working level, and you gain all the space under the benches for equipment, accessories, pots, flats, whatever.

We offer two basic types of good, long-lasting benches: one made of redwood lumber top and sides, the other of cement board top and redwood sides, both supported by a galvanized pipe framework. Each of these benches has 6 inch high sides to receive and hold soil for direct planting, or to hold potted plants . . . as you like.

Either way, benches allow you to maintain a close control over a plant's growing conditions, including its soil mix (if planted directly in a bench) and drainage. Both kinds of bench will have holes or horizontal openings to allow excess water to drain out. Benches make greenhouse gardening more convenient and less time-consuming. You can do your daily chores without constantly bending or stretching to reach all of your plants. And they are all clearly in sight, allowing you to keep a close watch for signs of trouble. And, of course, they add to your display of beauty and your enjoyment of green life.

Benches must be carefully constructed in order to withstand weight and large amounts of water. "Composistion board," made of cement and asbestos fiber, is often used to construct bench tops. Redwood, because of its resistance to rot, is also frequently used. A framework of galvanized iron pipes has often been used to support the bench.

A bench with sides can be used to hold either a potting medium, or pots. Or, you can also make or purchase a bench without sides, intended for use only as a support for pots. Holes drilled in the bottom of the board, or horizontal openings, are used to get rid of excess water. Some benches also have openings along the sides through which water can flow.

You may wish to make your own benches. If you are handy with tools, there is no reason why you shouldn't. However, many greenhouse manufacturers also make aand market a variety of benches. Some of the benches are designed to be used in either of their capacities — others can be used only for one or the other purposes. They are available in a wide range of sizes and prices.

Many kinds of plants can also be grown **under** a bench, thus increasing the amount of growing space in your unit. Because they will be catching some of the water coming out of the bench, you will have to select plants for such a location carefully. Of course, a plant appreciating frequent waterings will probably do best. Also, choose such plants on the basis of how much light is available under the benches.

Because benches are large and heavy, you must carefully determine where they should be placed in advance. Many greenhouses have benches running along both walls, with perhaps a smaller bench along an end wall. Some greenhouse owners prefer to have benches built into the unit, actually attached to the walls. This precludes any other arrangement. No matter how large your unit is, space is always strictly limited. So before you build or buy your benches, sit down and try out some alternate designs.

Your arrangement of plants on a bench can also be a factor in exploiting space. Group plants by their shared species, or by their shared needs (plants requiring frequent watering in one spot, or plants in the same growth stage). Within each grouping, arrange the plants according to their size and size of their pots. Keep smaller plants towards the outer side, larger plants toward the back. You may find that such a careful arrangement will simplify your procedures and may also conserve space, allowing you to include additional plants.

I know of one woman who runs her greenhouse without using even one bench. She plants her entire collection into a specially prepared soil mix, applied to a depth of six inches over the unit's floor. She cultivates only cacti, and she has arranged them in such a skillful way that, upon entering the unit, you might think you had walked into a miniature desert. Such an arrangement, however, is highly unusual. Most of us need benches.

SHELVES

Shelves are a useful addition to any greenhouse because they create new growing space at a·modest cost. You can place the shelves, singly or in tiers, in several corners of your unit. In a lean-to, you can attach long shelves to the back wall of the unit. And if you have a spot too small to contain a shelf, install a wall bracket to support one plant. Space is always at a premium in a greenhouse, and anything you can do to increase the growing area is well worth the effort.

You can purchase shelves from a number of sources, including some greenhouse manufacturers, or you can make them yourself. Use boards at least ¾″ thick, and use rust-resistant fixtures to hold the shelves in place. Redwood, because of its resistance to moisture or warping, would prove an excellent wood for shelves. You can now purchase sheets of preforated aluminum for use as shelves. And you might even use glass, or strongly supported plastic, for shelves. Glass or plastic, while fragile, have the positive feature of allowing light to fall through them onto plants below.

Fill your shelves with small plants that might do badly if they are overshadowed by larger plants on a bench. Trailing plants do well — and look good — grown on shelves. Or reserve a shelf for growing just cacti. Because the corners of a unit tend to be warmer than the center of a unit, you can grow many types of warmth-loving plants on a shelf. Reserve a particularly sunny corner for sun-loving plants. Small flats of seelings will also do well in such a location.

Because greenhouses are so confined, it often seems as if every element of the unit affects every other element. If you add shelves, make certain that they don't prevent necessary sunlight from falling upon plants below. And check to be sure that the excess of water draining from pots on shelves is not causing a problem for the plants positioned around and below the shelves. Continuous dripping can encourage rots in a plant or even damage tender leaves.

By all means, if you can add shelves to your unit, do so.

POTS

You will probably need pots for your greenhouse. How many you will need depends on the number of plants you have, the number of plants you plan to propagate and the method of gardening you have adopted. Some gardeners grow their plants directly in the benches. Personally, I prefer to grow most plants in individual containers. I believe that growing plants in separate pots gives you greater mobility, allowing you to move plants to other areas of your unit. It also simplifies watering your collection. Remember that different species of plants have different watering requirements. When you are dealing with potted plants, you can give each plant the amount of water it needs, at the intervals it prefers. However, when you must water an entire bench, you have to compromise and evenly apply an average amount of water. Is it ever advisable to grow plants directly in a bench? Yes, if you are growing a number of the same type and size of plant, in which case they will have the same requirements. Also, a bench or a portion of a bench used as a propagating area would have a uniform watering requirement.

If you purchase your first plants for the greenhouse from any plant outlet, the plants will be in a pot. However, if friends make gifts of small plants or cuttings to help begin your collection, you may have to have pots on hand to receive the donations. I suggest you purchase a **small** stock of pots to have on hand, when you begin gardening. Perhaps half a dozen pots, in several sizes, should be enough of a reserve when you begin working in your greenhouse. As your collection increases (through additional gifts or through propagation), and as mature plants outgrow their present pots, you will then have occasion to purchase an additional supply.

Pots are available in a wide range of sizes, beginning at 2½″ and going up to 15″ in diameter. The depth of a standard pot is equal to its diameter at the rim. Most pots are made of either clay or plastic. There has been a long, if mild, debate among gardeners as to which material is preferable. I personally don't think there is much of a contest. Each type has its advantages and disadvantages.

Clay pots are manufactured in just one shade — the familiar earthy red. Plastic pots are available in a variety of colors.

Plastic pots are lighter than clay pots — but, if you have a topheavy plant, you had better use a clay pot to anchor it.

Clay pots are more fragile. Plastic pots are quite durable.

Water evaporates through the walls of a clay pot, as well as from the soil surface, which means that a plant will receive an even distribution of water.

Water evaporates only from the surface of a plastic pot. Moisture is retained longer in the soil, which is helpful for a plant requiring constant moisture, but a drawback if you water too much. Water might accumulate, and there is a chance of rot. In a clay pot, water would not accumulate in such a way.

My suggestion is to keep some of each on hand. No matter which you buy, inspect every pot before you purchase it to be certain that it has a drainage hole (or holes) in its base, to allow excess water to escape. Pots lacking such holes are of no use in a greenhouse, and can prove harmful to plants. With no exit, the excess of water that occurs after any watering would simply remain in the bottom of the pot, smothering the roots or encouraging a rot to settle in.

Saucers are available to match any size pot. Placed under a pot, they are removed and drained of the excess water they receive from the plant after each watering. However, you don't need saucers in a greenhouse because your benches will have a sufficient number of holes to carry away the water excess. You may, however, want to use saucers for pots you have placed on shelves, to prevent water from spilling haphazardly onto the plants below.

There is no way to get around your need for pots. Fortunately, they are not expensive. And, if you clean them carefully, you can use them again and again.

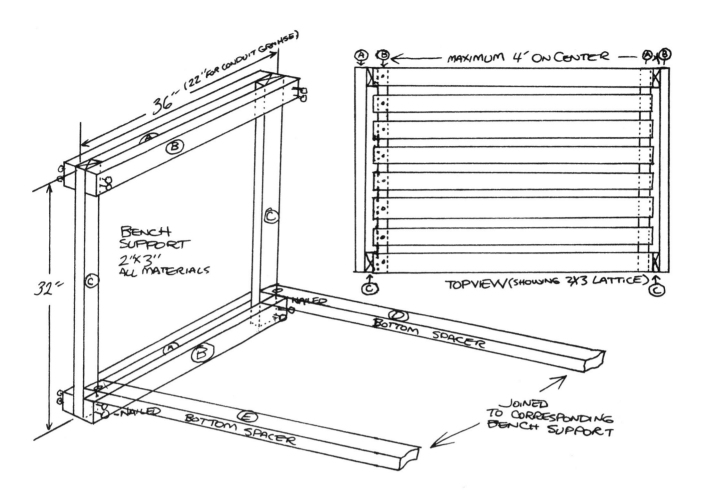

36" (22" FOR CONDUIT GRNHSE)

MAXIMUM 4' ON CENTER

BENCH SUPPORT 2"×3" ALL MATERIALS

32"

Ⓐ Ⓑ

Ⓒ

NAILED

BOTTOM SPACER

NAILED

BOTTOM SPACER

TOPVIEW (SHOWING 2×3 LATTICE)

JOINED TO CORRESPONDING BENCH SUPPORT

Design for Potting Bench

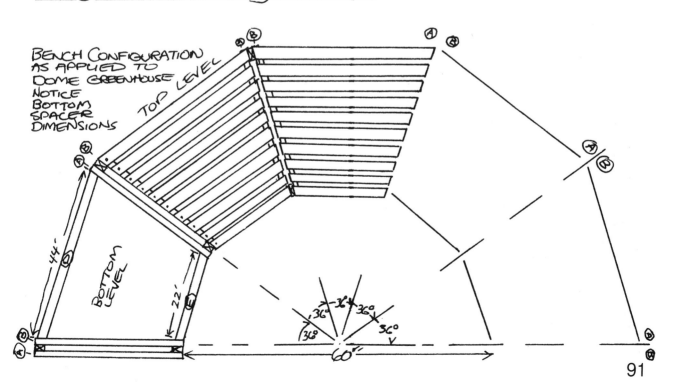

BENCH CONFIGURATION AS APPLIED TO DOME GREENHOUSE NOTICE BOTTOM SPACER DIMENSIONS

TOP LEVEL

BOTTOM LEVEL

44"

22"

60"

36° 36° 36° 36°

Chapter 12.
AVOIDING PROBLEMS

The manner in which you run your greenhouse can greatly affect the frequency and seriousness of the infections and insect infestations that can strike your plants. In any greenhouse, no matter how carefully it is tended, there are going to be some losses due to insects or some disease. But occasional losses, while they are disturbing, happen to everyone who works with plants. I have never met a gardener who hasn't lost at least one plant to aphids, or mites, or root rot. However, the more diligent you are, the less likely it is that you will lose any considerable number of plants.

If you do not keep your greenhouse clean, such debris as decaying organic matter will attract and act as safe haven for many kinds of pests. And if you do not regularly inspect your plants and the entire unit for signs of bug activity, you may not discover their presence until they have caused considerable damage.

You must not only keep your unit clean — you must see that its systems are properly adjusted and functioning. That is, you must not allow the temperature to fluctuate widely. The unit should have sufficient ventilation to keep the air from becoming stagnant. The humidity level should remain stable and rather high, especially during the summer. If any of the systems malfunction, or if you neglect to regulate them, your plants can become traumatized, and thus susceptible to infection or attack.

These responsibilities sound a good deal more time-consuming than they are. If you establish a regular daily schedule for watering, feeding and inspecting your plants, and if you are careful to keep the unit clean, you should find greenhouse gardening a pleasant and constantly rewarding activity. It's only when carelessness or bad luck force you to deal with a serious problem that you wonder **why** you ever took up gardening in a greenhouse.

So follow a regular schedule. Keep a close eye on your plants for any symptoms of trouble. And when trouble does occur — don't panic. This chapter describes the commonest plant pests and diseases, their symptoms and a variety of remedies. Once you have learned to identify symptoms of trouble, you can often act quickly to treat a problem before it becomes severe. Many treatments are simple and, as long as you observe some basic precautions when working with chemicals, entirely safe.

But remember, if you keep your unit clean, many of the worst problems should pass you by.

Now what exactly is it that you must clean? After each potting session, or after each watering or feeding, there may be some spilled soil, dirt shards of crockery or spilled liquids on your work area. I have found that, if I don't clean up such things immediately, it may be some time before I get back to it. So clean it up as soon as you have finished the procedure, and dispose immediately of anything that is not reusable (potting soil is **not** reusable — if it has been used once, throw it out).

Clean your tools as soon as you have finished using them. Don't leave containers of soil or fertilizer to stand open — close them as soon as you have taken out what you need. If, after a transplanting procedure, you are left with one or several empty pots, scrub them and soak pots immediately, and store them where they will be in reach but out of the way of a careless elbow.

Your most important housekeeping chore is to keep the growing area clean. Clear away dead foliage from the soil surface of plants and from the benches, as soon as you spot such debris. If soil has spilled out of the pots or benches, sweep it up and discard it immediately. Try not to stand unused pots or crockery close to the plants, as such receptacles often serve as home for nocturnal insects. Check every day for such small things, and clean them up as you find them.

Make cleaning a regular feature of your gardening schedule. As with most other aspects of greenhouse gardening, your common sense is the best guide. If you take a good look at the unit, you'll **know** what you have to do.

Once a year, give your unit a thorough cleaning. I believe the summer is the most convenient time for such a project, because you can move plants outdoors without exposing them to harsh weather. Don't put the plants in direct sunlight — keep them in a shaded area. When you bring them back in to the just-cleaned unit, check them all for any insects that may be hitching a ride.

Begin by removing all of the pots or containers stored under the benches, and any plants kept there. Then empty the benches. If you use the benches to hold potted plants, you can quickly and easily move the plants outside. If you have plants growing directly in the benches, you cannot remove them. But you can take this occasion to thoroughly turn all of the soil, to mix in fresh soil and even to add a dose of fertilizer.

Take down any hanging baskets, and if you use shelves clear them of plants. After all of the plants have been removed, scrub everything — benches, shelves and walls, with warm soapy water and a stiff brush. Then thoroughly rinse all of the surfaces with a strong stream of water.

If your unit is in need of any repairs, this is the time to do it. Perhaps some of the plastic skin has cracked and must be replaced. Or some putty is missing from a glass panes. Check all of the unit's appliances, to make sure that they function, and that the electrical wiring is not defective or worn.

Now bring your plants back in. As you do, you may discover new ways of arranging the unit. And you may also discover pots or containers that are no longer of any use. Take this opportunity to examine all of your plants, all of your containers and tools and the unit itself for any problems or damage.

Such thorough housekeeping is one part of running an effective, productive greenhouse. This work can help to keep your plants healthy. In the long run, energy expended in this area can save you grief.

But what if, despite all your precautions, a plant falls ill (as one of your plants, sometime, is bound to.) What's gone wrong, and what's going on?

PESTS

You are going to have insects in your greenhouse. You will certainly have them your first summer in the greenhouse, and you will probably find pests returning as regularly as the seasons thereafter. No matter how diligent you are, no matter how exhaustive your precautions, some insects are bound to slip in. They may crawl through some crack or aperture so small you could not know of its existence. They may fly in. They may enter clinging to a gardening tool, concealed in a load of soil, or even clutching some fold of your clothes. Insects **will** get in. And you will have to act quickly and efficiently to prevent serious damage to your plants.

Throughout the spring and summer you will have to keep a close, daily watch for signs of insects. You will have to be especially thorough in keeping the greenhouse clean, in order and free of debris. And you will have to become familiar with the procedures for handling insect attacks once they occur, so that you can end an insect infestation before it becomes severe.

Don't depend on visually spotting a crawling or flying insect. Many species are masters of concealment, and others are so small that they can just about be perceived by the unaided eye. Still others use camouflage to blend into plant surfaces. The first sure sign of an insect infestation will be destruction and decay. Leaves may suddenly turn yellow or brown. Jagged holes may appear in foliage. Plant growth may slow, or even stop as the plant wilts badly. Some insects smear a honeydew-like substance over leaves or stem — that substance serves both to attact ants, which carry the bugs excreting the substance from plant to plant, like a six-legged Typhoid Mary, and as a medium for the growth of damaging, unsightly molds. Tiny bumps may appear on a plant's stem where before the stem had been smooth and unmarked. Small, coarse cobwebs may noticeably span a plant's leaf axils.

What should you do when you notice any of these symptoms? If the insects are large enough (such as snails or slugs) you can simply lift them off and take them outside. Holding a plant under a strong stream of lukewarm water will dislodge some types of insects. Carefully scrubbing each plant part may be required to get rid of some other types of pests. Relatively mild pesticides, such as Malathion or Rotenone, are sufficient to end most insect attacks, and to repel any further infestations. Only for the most persistent or damaging of insects should you consider using a very strong pesticide. Never, never reach for the poison as soon as you believe some insects are present. Identify the species, and then check to discover which treatment will be most effective against them. You may be amazed to discover that surprisingly simple treatments are sufficient to handle many bug attacks.

You **are** going to have insects in your greenhouse. But by keeping your unit clean and free of debris, and by regularly inspecting it for signs of insect activity, you can greatly decrease the chance of a serious attack. By becoming familiar with the signs of an insect attack, and with the treatments you can apply, you can reduce the time and effort involved in ending an insect attack, and you can reduce the damage to your plants.

This section includes a description of the signals and appearance of each of the most commonly occuring plant pests. In addition, various treatments are listed for dealing with each insect. The sight of a damaged plant or of pests moving freely about is enough to concern any greenhouse gardener. But if you keep your head, don't overreact, and match the treatment to the pest, you should be able to spare yourself any serious losses.

APHIDS

Aphids are tiny, pear shaped insects that are really noticeable only during a very close inspection of a plant. Their soft bodies may be red, black or green.

Aphids damage a plant by piercing its tissue and sucking out the vital sap. They most often cluster around a plant's stems and its newly budded terminal leaves. Curled or puckered leaves, a spindly stem or a sudden decline in the growth rate are all symptoms of an aphid attack. Aphids also excrete a honeydew-like substance that you may find smeared upon the leaf surfaces. The young of some species of aphids shelter within galls, or bumps that appear upon the plant. The young feed on the plant, protected by the shell of the swollen tissue, and emerge when they are mature to seek out a new food supply.

If only one or a few plants have been attacked, you can thoroughly rinse each of them in warm soapy water, being sure to wash the undersides of all the leaves and growing tip-ends. Any badly discolored foliage, or seriously infested stems or leaves, should be cut off and discarded

immediately. Don't let diseased parts lay in the open on your work area. Put them in a closed container or take them outside as soon as you have pared them off.

Isolate all of the plants having any symptoms of an aphid infestation. Spraying them with Malathion diluted in water should also help to end the attack. If you suspect other plants on the same bench **might** be in danger, spray them with Malathion as well. Don't take chances; it is always better to be on the side of caution.

If a plant has been so weakened by the loss of its sap that it is dying, take cuttings of any uninfested parts and then discard the rest of the plant. Wash them and spray them with Malathion before rooting them.

ANTS

While ants rarely damage plants directly, their presence in a greenhouse can be quite troublesome. They act as carriers for mealybugs, scale and aphids, literally carrying these destructive pests on their backs from location to location. It seems that ants have a real fondness for the sticky honeydew-like substance that these bugs excrete. Ants may also inadvertently introduce fungus or bacterial infections. Their burrowing activities are unsightly and may disturb and damage a plant's roots. And they are capable of carrying off the seeds that you have so recently, carefully planted in expectation of a crop of new plants.

Because ant eggs may be concealed in unsterilized soil, you can reduce the possibility of their presence in your unit by using only sterilized soil. As ants may be attracted by piles of decaying organic matter, such as dead plant leaves or stems, you must keep your work and growing areas free of such debris.

If an ant mound springs up on your greenhouse floor, or if you find a number of these bugs industriously exploring the growing areas, you will have to take action. Pour Malathion on the ant mound. Drench the soil of any plant suffering from ant activity with Malathion dissolved in water.

Tansy, a common herb, has an aroma that seems to repel ants. You might want to experiment by planting tansy around the door and along the sides of your unit.

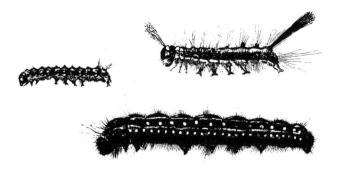

CATERPILLARS

Caterpillars are the immature form of moths and butterflies. These wormlike pests rapaciously devour huge quantities of buds, flowers and leaves, and can defoliate a plant in a very short span of time. While

they should not be a major problem in your greenhouse, an occasional caterpillar may enter concealed in soil brought in from your yard, or clinging to a tool or some fold of your clothing.

You may spot a caterpillar while it is at work, tearing great holes in a plant's foliage or flowers. However, many species emerge to feed only at night, carefully concealing themselves during the day from predators. If they are nocturnal feeders, you will notice jagged holes appearing in foliage overnight, and you may also find the numerous black specks of their excrement dotting leaves. If your plants have any of these symptoms, inspect them for caterpillars. Check the undersides of leaves for a drip concealed caterpillar, groupings of young caterpillars or patches of eggs. Cut such infested leaves off immediately, and destroy them. Isolate any damaged plants, and keep an eye on them for several days, for any signs of new activity.

You can also soak the soil of an infested plant with Malathion, and apply a spray of Malathion to the foliage. Caterpillars prefer dark, protected hiding places, such as under pots, so if you are having trouble you may have to work your way through an entire bench in a hunt for hidden caterpillars. They may also be attracted to piles of decaying organic matter, so **keep your unit clean**. A clean greenhouse is, I think, much less susceptible to attacks of many species of insects.

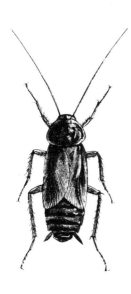

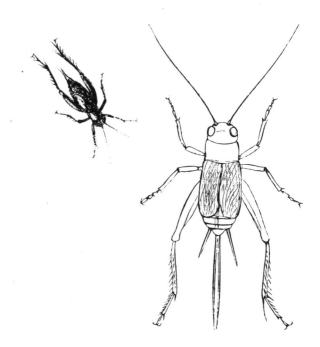

COCKROACHES

Cockroaches are such familiar pests that they require no description. An occasional cockroach may wander into your greenhouse, and he may stay to feed on the leaves of your plants. Ragged leaf edges, or missing tip ends are the signs of a cockroach attack.

As cockroaches are usually active only at night, you may have to make a nighttime inspection of your unit to locate them. During the day they will conceal themselves in dark, obscure places. Remove any roaches that you find. If one or two plants have been repeatedly attacked, spray the foliage with a preparation of Malathion and water. You may also place roach powders in one or two spots that seems to be frequented by the roaches — but I don't recommend making a habit of this. Only use chemicals of any sort as you need them — and even then, sparingly — and then put them away.

If you keep your greenhouse clean and free of debris, you can reduce the likelihood of a serious cockroach problem.

CRICKETS

Crickets may do little harm in your garden, but in your greenhouse they can cause real trouble. Given the opportunity, they will gladly feed on the leaves and flowers of plants, vegetables and seedlings. If a plant's small, new leaves disappear overnight, suspect crickets. They move about at night, and spend the days hiding in whatever small, dark havens they can find. As with so many other insects, they are attracted to decaying organic matter.

If you find crickets moving about, get rid of them. If a plant is being repeatedly attacked, treat the soil with Malathion dissolved in water.

It is difficult, if not impossible, to locate concealed insects. To control nocturnal insects, you are probably going to have to spend some time in your unit at night, looking for and getting rid of them. It cannot be stressed too heavily that a constantly clean greenhouse will attract and harbor fewer bugs, making pest control much easier and decreasing the chance of any real harm to your plants.

CUTWORMS

Cutworms are a destructive form of moth larvae. The moth lays its eggs on spears of grass or weeds, and after hatching, the worms burrow into the ground. As they grow they develop soft, smooth, large bodies. Cutworms often take shelter in the soil just below the surface. At night they emerge to feed on plant stems close to the ground. Cutworms are capable of slashing right through a stem, causing a plant to collapse, or their feeding may damage it badly but leave it upright. The damaged plant will then wilt and die. Some species of cutworms actually crawl up the stem, and feed on leaves and flowers. Working inward from the margins, they will chew large irregular holes in the foliage. Cutworms are especially dangerous because they will partially slash through stem after stem, badly damaging many plants but killing few outright.

Cutworms may be introduced to your unit in a number of ways. Eggs might be carried in concealed in unsterilized soil, or an individual or several cutworms might find some other means of entering. If a plant looks like a cutworm has attacked, it will probably be too late to save it. But you can take action to save the rest of your plants. You can hand pick any larvae that emerge at night. You can gently turn over the soil around a plant, as the cutworms often remain quite near the surface.

You can also apply a Malathion drench to the soil. Again, taking some basic precautions should lessen the problem. Use sterilized soil. Inspect all your tools used in outdoor gardening before you bring them into your unit. If you detect any damage, investigate immediately.

EARWIGS

Earwigs are dark brown insects resembling beetles. They are a little less than an inch long, but they can be readily identified by a tail appendage resembling a pair of forceps. They are nocturnal creatures, emerging at night to feed on leaves, flowers and ripening fruits. Earwigs are most common in the costal states.

Small holes in flowers or leaves often are the first sign of an earwig attack. Spraying the foliage of a plant with Malathion should end any attack.

Long before they had chemicals, gardeners and farmers were dealing with earwigs quite successfully. Their method makes shrewd use of the earwigs preference for dark, dry places during the day. Flowerpots or other containers, with dry moss pressed to their sides and base, and inverted and placed on sticks about a garden. The earwigs, after a night of feeding, will be attracted to the containers as a comfortable refuge. Every morning, the containers were collected, and submerged in water or kerosene. I know of at least one gardener today who claims he is successfully dealing with earwigs by using matchboxes.

The most lethal treatment is not necessarily always the best.

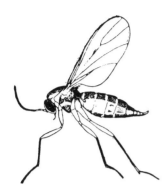

FUNGUS GNATS

Fungus gnats are those gray or sooty black dots that can often be seen hovering about a plant's foliage or the soil. While they in themselves are harmless, the eggs they lay on the soil soon hatch into tiny burrowing maggots. These maggots attack root tissue, causing scars or even consuming entire small roots. An infested plant will cease growing and will wilt without identifiable cause. In addition, the wounds in the roots may serve as an entrance to root rot or some other disease.

The presence of the adults will indicate the problem. You can use an aerosol pesticide spray to deal with the egg-laying adults — but only use a spray that specifically states that it can be used without harm around plants. Try not to spray the plant itself. Isolate all the plants showing symptoms of infection, and immerse them overnight in a container of water. The water level should be just above the soil line, which will cause numbers of the maggots to drown. Because these gnats live for only a few weeks before a new generation emerges,

they may prove to be a stubborn problem. Each time you notice adults, you will have to immerse the plant in water again. A solution of Malathion and water may also be applied to the soil. Eventually, the gnats will be exterminated.

Fungus gnats prefer to breed in damp environments, so be sure to examine your watering procedure, to be certain that you are not giving your plants too much water.

LEAFMINERS

Leafminers are an infrequent problem, but when they do appear they can cause serious damage. They are the larval form of several kinds of flies, sawflies and moths. They will work their way into the interior of a leaf and, once safely protected between its surfaces, they will proceed to chew away the interior tissue. They create winding tunnels as they feed, causing a leaf to appear as if it is striped or mined with bands lighter than the rest of the tissue. Hence their name — leafminers.

Badly infested leaves soon wilt and drop off. Some leaves may simply yellow or turn brown — but the effect of a leafminer attack is distinctive, and its tunnels cannot be mistaken for any other problem.

It is difficult to treat them, as they are protected by their host when they are causing the worst damage. Cut off and destroy all leaves that appear infested. Isolate the plant, and apply a spray of either Malathion or Rotenone dissolved in water.

99

LEAFROLLERS

Leafrollers are a type of caterpillar — the larval form of moths. They are named by their practice of rolling a leaf protectively around them as they feed.

If leaves on a plant appear to be tightly rolled up, straighten them and examine the interior. You may find a leafroller at work, taking bites out of the leaf. Or you may find a bundle of overlapping flattened green droplets — the leafroller's eggs. Pick off any individuals, and destroy all rolled leaves, in case an egg bundle may be concealed on it. Spray the remainder of the foliage with Malathion. Sevin, a systemic poison, is also said to be effective in controlling a leafroller infestation. However, systemics are very powerful poisons, and should be used only as a last resort, I believe. (see the section on pesticides)

MEALYBUGS

Mealybugs are one of the commonest and most troublesome of plant pests. These tiny bugs gather to form powdery masses on leaf axils and stem joints. They have soft, segmented ovular bodies. Filaments of a white waxy substance extend from all portions of their tiny bodies. The females are very prolific, producing as many as 600 eggs at one time. Both young and adult mealybugs feed by piercing plant tissue with sharp beaks and sucking out the sap.

Mealybugs excrete a honeydew-like substance that attracts ants and acts as a medium for the growth of a sooty mold. The first sign of a mealybug attack may be the noticeable decline of a plant, as it wilts and visibly weakens. The sticky substance, or the cottony bunting should identify the problem.

You can pick clumps of the bugs off by hand, but you will probably miss some of them. Even one stray female can repopulate a plant in short order. A popular remedy calls for dabbing each bug with a cotton swab that has been dipped in denatured alcohol. The alcohol penetrates the filaments and kills the bug. However, it is tedious work, and the residue of alcohol left on a plant after this treatment could, possibly, harm it.

Remove any mealybugs you see, and spray the plant with Malathion. Because their waxy filaments deflect water, washing a plant under attack will have no result.

Isolate any plant on which you discover mealybugs. You might even want to give a preventitive spraying of Malathion to all the surrounding plants.

MILLIPEDES

Millipedes are often referred to as having a "thousand legs." In fact, they have only 30 to 40 pairs. Millipedes have cylindrical, hard-shelled, many-segmented bodies and they average an inch in length. They also have a short pair of segmented antennae.

You can find millipedes coiled in rich soil or decaying organic material. When they are disturbed they can move quite rapidly. Outdoors they scavenge for organic wastes, and they prey on some small insects. They may also eat seeds, young roots or the stems of seedlings. If one enters your greenhouse, it could cause considerable trouble in your propagation bench or flat.

While millipedes are nocturnal feeders, they rarely go far from plants during the day. If you suspect their presence, probe the soil around your plants. Because of their fondness for organic materials, you should thoroughly check any soil having a concentration of humus or peat moss. And if you have left any plant debris about, it will provide a home for many types of insects, including millipedes.

Pick off and discard any millipedes you discover. Drench the soil of a vulnerable or damaged plant with a solution of Malathion. Millipedes have a reputation for being serious, stubborn pests, so you must keep a watch for any signs of their presence, and take action as soon as you determine that they are at work.

NEMATODES

Nematodes are the focus of a widespread debate. Some entomologists and agricultural specialists insist on classifying them as a disease, while others regard them as an insect. The disagreement centers over whether the bugs actually damage plants, or simply serve to introduce diseases into the root system.

If you use only sterilized soil, you should not have to worry about this admittedly serious problem. Even if you don't plan to use sterilized soil in your unit, I suggest that you contact your local agricultural officer. If nematodes are a frequent problem in your area, you really should spend the extra money on sterile soil. For nematodes are miscroscopic wormlike creatures that can rarely be detected until the damage has been done. Roots affected by nematodes will develop knots or balls, become shrunken and finally die. With them, of course, goes the plant.

If a plant suddenly stops growing, or if its foliage becomes wilted or drops off, examine the roots. If the roots appear to be badly diseased, it will be best to discard the plant and examine all the plants nearby for nematodes. Scour everything that has come into contact with the plant, including tools, your work area, even your clothes and hands, as nematodes are tremendously infectious.

The solution V-C-13 is said to be effective in controlling nematode attacks, and you might want to treat nearby plants with it. While there are preparations designed for use specifically against nematodes, they are really only for use outdoors, and may not be effective in your greenhouse.

SCALE

Scale can cause serious damage to a plant before you ever suspect their presence. They resemble tiny bumps, and can easily be mistaken for the natural protuberances of a plants stem. However, they may also be found attached to the underside of leaves. If a number of scale are present, they may cluster together, in which case you will be sure to notice the unusual grouping of bumps. If you look closely you will see that their shells have a waxy texture, and if you prod one with a fingernail you will find that the bug is quite soft underneath its semi-hard shell.

Scale suck the sap out of a plant, causing leaves to become spotted, turn yellow and even drop off. An entire plant may wilt and fail under a scale attack. Scale also secrete a sticky substance that attracts ants. Indeed, ants are so fond of the stuff that they willingly carry scale about on their backs from plant to plant. Citrus and avocado plants seem especially attractive to scale.

Wash an infested plant in warm soapy water — but **don't** use a detergent. As you apply the water, gently but firmly run your fingers over the stem and leaves. The scale will readily fall off. Rinse the plant in clear lukewarm water, and repeat the process once or twice more, at intervals of several days. You can also spray the foliage with Malathion.

Try to regularly inspect all of your plants. If you do, you can prevent some insect attacks and reduce the harm of others. If you rarely make it a habit to look closely at your plants as you water or tend them, you may find the number of plants lost to insects or diseases steadily increasing.

SNAILS, SLUGS

Snails and slugs are familiar residents of most gardens, but they have no place in a greenhouse. While only a few of the many species of snails and slugs feed on plants, you should not assume that the snail inching along the greenhouse floor is one of the harmless varieties. Pick up any snails or slugs you discover in your unit and return them to their accustomed home — the outdoors.

Snails have soft, unsegmented bodies protected by hard, humped shells. When threatened, they can entirely withdraw into the shell. Slugs are shelles snails. Most slugs and snails are nocturnal feeders, and those kinds that feed on plants rasp large, ragged holes in foliage. While the torn leaves may not positively identify the pest involved, both snails and slugs leave a tell-tale slimy trail behind them. Snails, and especially the fat, defenseless slugs carefully conceal themselves during the day in dark places, such as in piles of debris or under pots.

Many gardeners use a "folk remedy" that, remarkably, seems to do the job. They sink a jar lid of beer (stale or fresh) or fermented grape juice into the soil surface of a plant that has been previously attacked. Emerging after dark, the snails or slugs will be attracted to the liquid and, incredibly, often fall in and drown. Slugs can be discouraged from entering an area by placing bits of crockery, sharp pebbles or sand around the areas margins. Slugs avoid anything that can bruise their unshielded flesh.

If the problem is severe, potent baits can be used. They must be placed in an area frequented by the bugs, but they must also be partially concealed under a jar lid or a piece of wood. The idea is to discourage prying paws or tiny hands, for the poison is very strong, but still allow snails or slugs to approach. However, baits should rarely be necessary.

SOWBUG

Sowbug is a name used to identify several types of plant pests. Sowbugs have flat, oval bodies, 7 pairs of legs, are brown and average about ½'' in length. One type of sowbug — the pillbug — curls itself into a pill-like ball whenever it is alarmed.

They prefer damp locations, and are also attracted to decaying organic materials, such as soil, compost or fallen leaves or stems. Sowbugs primarily harm seedlings, as they will feed on their stems or roots. If your seedlings wilt, grow noticeably slower or lose their leaves, keep the possibility of a sowbug attack in mind as you investigate. Check any areas within the unit that are often damp. Inspect under pots or other containers. And poke gently about the soil around the seedlings.

If you discover any, pick them off and destroy them. It is unusual to suffer a major sowbug attack — most often, only one or a few individuals are present.

The soil of threatened or damaged plants may also be treated with a solution of water and Malathion.

SPIDER MITES

Spider mites are real trouble. They can kill a plant so fast that you'll still be wondering what hit it after it is dead.

They are not true insects, but relatives of the spider family. They have unsegmented bodies and three pairs of legs, but you may never know that, for they are incredibly small. The female of one species is an average of 1/50th of an inch long, and she is larger than the male at that! However, if you use a magnifying glass to study them (a handy tool for a greenhouse gardener) you will be able to see their oval bodies attached to various parts of a plant.

The first sign of an attack may be the tiny, coarse webs that the mites spin across the underside of a leaf, on a terminal leaf or, quite frequently, across a leaf axil. The mites use their sharp sucking mouth parts to pierce plant tissue and draw out the sap.

As they are literally sucked dry, leaves will become mottled, or be marked by blotches of grey. Leaves may wilt, and some may fall off. Mites will not give up a plant until it is near to death.

At the first sign, at the first **hint** of an infestation isolate the plant or plants. Mites are nastily contagious, passing from plant to plant by means of a tool, or even your hands. Scour everything that comes into contact with the plant.

Hold the plant under a forceful stream of water. This will dislodge and sweep away many of the mites and their webs. Repeat the procedure every few days for a week or two. Give an infested plant's neighbors the same treatment at least once, to clear off any mites before they have a chance to make themselves at home.

Ced-O-Flora, a spray made from petroleum, cedar and hemlock oils and soap is often helpful in controlling an attack. It should be mixed in water and sprayed on the undersides of leaves and around leaf axils. Malathion may also be used on mites.

roots, root hairs and submerged plant stems. The damaged roots will be unable to draw in sufficient water or nutrients, and a plant attacked by a symphylan will wilt and even fail.

Symphylans generally enter a greenhouse in unpasteurized soil. Once in, they will be attracted to any organic debris laying about. By using sterilized soil, and keeping all work areas clean, you can reduce the chance of a symphylan attack.

Because the symphylan is so rarely seen, it may destroy a plant before you have figured out the baffling symptoms of trouble. If you suspect an attack, turn the plant out, examine the roots for signs of damage and sift through the soil. Cut off all damaged root tissue, and repot the plant in sterilized soil. You may also treat a symphylan attack by drenching the soil with Malathion. It may be that as you sift through the old soil, you will discover these tiny, white menaces desperately scrambling for cover. Remove any you find.

If a plant has been too badly injured to save, take cuttings from its remaining healthy parts and root them in sterile soil.

SYMPHYLAN

The symphylan, sometimes called the "garden centipede," is an especially destructive plant pest. Symphylans are very small (adults average ¼" long) and they have white, wormlike bodies and twelve pairs of legs. They are attracted to decaying organic matter, and frequently use such material as a hiding place. Symphylans may also take shelter in the soil, and they will gravitate towards a plant's root system. They feed on young

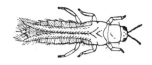

THRIPS

Thrips are very small, slender creatures that can just about be perceived moving about on a plant. Their rasping mouth parts saw away tissue, causing pockmarks and whitened streaks to appear, especially on the underside of leaves. Flower buds may fail to open and drop off. Some leaves may be so badly damaged as to develop a rough, papery texture. Blisters on a leaf indicate the points where female thrips have inserted eggs.

Washing a plant with lukewarm soapy water will end most thrip attacks. Malathion, sprayed at regular intervals over several days on the underside of leaves, will eliminate any stubborn hold-overs.

WHITE FLY

White flies are very tiny white flying insects that, upon close inspection, resemble moths more than they do flies. They are rarely in evidence on a plant until the plant is disturbed. Then, to your amazement, thick, compact white clouds will billow out of the plants foliage, hovering about until they can settle once again upon it — or, even more horrifying to a gardener, migrating to some other plant.

They gather in large groups on the underside of leaves, piercing the tissue to draw out the plant's sap. Leaves will soon yellow, wilt and fall off. The entire plant may wilt and cease growing. At a certain stage of their short lives white flies excrete a sticky matter that collects on leaves and forms a medium for a growth of a mold.

You can generally determine if a plant has white fly by shaking the foliage. An agitated white swarm will spring off the plant if it is. Their size, position on the plant and the speed with which they produce new generations makes them a difficult pest to eradicate.

Isolate all infested plants. Wash each of them with warm soapy (not detergent) water, scrubbing gently but thoroughly along the underside of all the leaves. Rinse the plant with clear water. Allow the plant to dry, then spray the foliage with Malathion. You may have to repeat the process several times, at intervals of several days, until the flies are completely absent.

Systemic pesticides are also said to be quite effective in ending white fly infestations.

Lantana and fuchsia are so attractive to white fly that they almost seem to produce the pest themselves. If you have had a difficult time ending an infestation, you might consider disposing of your lantana or fuchsia and concentrating on other plants. That may not be an easy decision, but white fly could potentially cause havoc in a greenhouse, and you must do everything you can to keep them out.

A WORD ON GENERATIONS

Most insects have what seem to us to be extraordinarily short, but prolific, life cycles. Aphids, for instance, have a one month lifecycle, and then die. But during that month each female produces several broods of up to thirty young. They in turn mature in ten to twelve days, and begin producing **more** young. A female spider mite can lay half a dozen eggs a day. Because of this continual production of young, you must generally treat an infested plant several times before you can be certain that all of the bugs have been eliminated. The first time you may kill off the adults — but there may be large numbers of eggs just about to hatch. So keep an infested plant isolated for at least a week after you begin treatment, and during that time repeat at least twice your procedure for clearing out the infestation.

AN ISOLATION WARD FOR YOUR PLANTS

As soon as you detect any signs of trouble, remove and isolate a plant from its bench or shelf mates. You may want to keep it on the work area, or you may want to reserve a shelf for infested or infected plants. If space is at a premium in your unit — as is so often the case — you may have to move a badly troubled plant out altogether, into your home or a work shed. But you should try to establish some area as a ward for suffering plants. Separating them should

also make it easier to give them the care they will need. In many cases it is also a good idea to give the plants surrounding an ill plant one dose of a pesticide or fungicide, depending on the problem. Inspect them closely throughout the following week for any signs of the trouble having passed on to them.

Friends

One of the drawbacks of the use of chemicals in the control of garden pests is the lethal nondiscrimination of the brews. They kill **anything** that comes into contact with them, regardless of whether the bug is a destructive pest or a harmless, or even helpful, resident of a garden. Recently, the practice of using bugs to control bugs has been receiving a great deal of attention, especially among organic gardeners committed to doing without any poisons. Such insects as the preying mantis, lady bug, spiders and some species of wasps feed on other insects, among them some of the most destructive of the plant pests, such as aphids, scale, mealybugs and spider mites. Lady bugs and the preying mantis have remarkable appetites, consuming daily many times their weight in plant-harming insects. Larger creatures, such as toads, frogs and, in some sections of the country, chameleons, also consume great number of insects with relish.

It is impractical to introduce any of these beneficial insects or reptiles into your unit, as can be done on a large scale by outdoor gardeners. But you should learn to distinguish the harmful insects from the helpful bugs, and if a friend shows up in your greenhouse, by all means don't disturb him. Leave him alone to go about his business, and he can be a real, though momentary, help to you. Toads, frogs or a chameleon may set up residence in your unit for an extended period of time, and that is all to the good. Lady bugs will not stay for any length of time, but spiders will. You may see few of these friends in your unit, but the chance of their presence, I think, is enough reason to refrain from blanketing the greenhouse with a fog of chemicals. Unless you have a really serious problem, use only what you need and apply it sparingly. Nature has its own balance in all things, and it is wise to disturb it as little as you can.

PLANT DISEASES

Plants become susceptible to diseases if they have received improper care, or if they have been placed in an unsuitable environment. For diseases do not attack healthy plants — they only settle on plants that have become weakened in some way, and thus are less able to resist infections.

As plant diseases are often the result of our mistakes, we can avoid plant loss due to infections by tending our plants carefully and satisfying their simple needs. Proper plant care, good sanitation and adequate ventilation help keep plants healthy, and healthy plants rarely fall victim to disease.

Match the plants you grow to the environment in which you intend to grow them. If you are running a cool greenhouse, for example, purchase or grow only those plants known to adapt to such an environment. **Use only sterilized soil.** Some gardeners believe such a precaution is unnecessary, but I do not. Unsterilized soil may contain the spores of many infections, only waiting for a proper chance to move into a plant's systems. Also, try not to expose your plants to sudden

fluctuations of temperatures, and protect them from drafts. Give a plant what it needs — a place in the sun, sufficient water and food — and it should do well. Deprive it of any of the basics, or give it too much of any of them, and you will weaken the plant, making it vulnerable to infection.

If a plant does exhibit some symptom of a disease, isolate it immediately. Keep it well separated from the rest of your plants. Examine the plant thoroughly, to determine the origin of the trouble, and the extent of the infection. Then see if you can discover how the problem started. Check your procedures to determine if you have been doing something wrong.

If the damage to the plant is extensive, (and some infections do spread devastatingly fast) take cuttings of any healthy plant parts and discard the rest. Don't keep a badly infected plant around, in an attempt to salvage it. It is always preferable to lose just one plant, rather than several. And in the close quarters of a greenhouse, an infection can spread with appalling speed.

Diseases need not to be a serious problem in your greenhouse. If you keep your unit clean, and give your plants what they need, infections may be a rare occurence, and cause only minor damage when they do appear.

What are the most frequently occuring plant diseases?

"Spot" Anthracnose is an infection characterized by visible depressions on a leaf, with each sunken spot having a raised rim. On some plants, the center of the spots will have a whitish color while the rim will be brown or black. Chinese evergreen, oleander and rubber plants all seem particularly susceptible to the disease. On rubber plants the infection first occurs as a bad burn on leaf tips, and then the entire edge of the leaf may yellow. Leaves fade until they are a withered brown.

Remove all the discolored leaves from the plant, and discontinue watering any infected plants until all signs of the problem have disappeared. While insects may introduce anthracnose to a plant, as may physical injury, it seems that excessive watering is a most frequent cause of the disease. If several of your plants have suffered from anthracnose, re-examine your watering practice. Perhaps you have been giving some of your plants too much water. Overwatering is an important factor in the appearence of many diseases, including funguses, molds and rots.

Bourdeaux mixture can be sprayed on the healthy leaves of a mildly infected plant, to keep the fungus from spreading.

BOTRYTIS

Botrytis is a fungus that is frequently fatal to African Violets. It occurs as a grayish-white mold that appears on the upper leaves of a plant. Attempting to grow too many Violets in too small a space, or providing them with inadequate ventilation seem to be the prime factors in its appearence.

Botrytis spreads rapidly. If a plant has patches of fungus on a number of its leaves, destroy it and immediately isolate all of its neighbors. Try to improve the ventilation in your unit, and don't keep plants so close that their foliage overlaps.

If botrytis has appeared on just a few leaves, remove those leaves and move the plant to a well ventilated, indirectly illuminated location. Because one touch is enough to transmit this killer to a plant, you must thoroughly wash your hands and any tools you have used immediately after you have worked on an infected plant.

Water a damaged plant only from the bottom up, and don't spray or mist the leaves. Be certain to keep the plant isolated until no new patches have appeared for at least a week.

CHLOROSIS

Chlorosis is a noncontagious deficiency disease that occurs in plants potted in a heavily alkaline soil. Too much alkalinity interferes with the plants ability to absorb such necessary nutrients as iron and the trace elements. Leaves that yellow while leaf veins remain green and a noticeable decline in the plant's growth rate indicate chlorosis.

The problem is easily remedied. Use a plant food having a high concentration of acid, or apply "chelated" iron to the soil. "Chelated" iron has been prepared in a form that plants can absorb without difficulty. I recommend the use of an acid-rich food, to insure that your plants are getting **all** of the nutrients they need, and not simply an increased supply of iron.

CROWN AND STEM ROT

A variety of fungus cause rot to settle in along stems and in a plant's crown. Excessive temperatures, or an excessive level of humidity in a greenhouse, without enough sunlight to make the humidity necessary, encourages rot. Continual overwatering and overmisting are prime causes of rot.

When a plant's stems or its crown become soft and pulpy, you will know that a rot is at work. Carefully consider the environmental conditions of a greenhouse, and correct any imbalances you discover. Cut out all of the damaged parts, and dust the cuts with a fungicide powder.

DAMPING-OFF DISEASE

Damping-off disease is a fungus that attacks seedlings, destroying stem and root tissue and causing the immature plant to collapse. It is invariably fatal.

Once damping-off disease has been introduced, it can quickly devastate an entire crop of seedlings, so you must try to keep it out. Because the disease travels in unsterilized soil, you can generally prevent it by planting your seedlings **only** in sterilized soil. Even if you don't use sterilized soil elsewhere in your unit, I urge you to use it here. I believe you will find the production of a healthy crop of seedlings well worth the minor expense of the soil.

If a seedling appears to be infected, remove it at once and treat the other seedlings around it with a fungicide dust. Excessive temperatures or levels of humidity seem to contribute to the appearence of the damping-off fungus. Remember, if damping-off appears, you may have a real problem on your hands. But you can greatly reduce the chance of your ever seeing the damping-off symptoms if you use sterilized soil.

LEAF SPOTS

Leaf spots are not a disease, but a symptom shared by many maladies. They may be caused by a disease, or by some unsettling factor in the environment. Leaf spots are well defined blotches on a leaf's surface, often having dark margins and white or brown centers. Spots may eventually cover an entire leaf, and badly spotted leaves may drop off.

Leaf spots tell you one of two things: that a plant is diseased, or that there is some imbalance in your unit's environment. However, an occasional spot is nothing to become seriously concerned about. If a number of leaves on a plant are spotted, you will have to investigate to discover what is wrong.

Is the plant (or plants) receiving enough light, or is it receiving too much? How often have you been watering it? Is there too much, or too little, humidity in the unit?

If the environment seems to be in balance, check the plant for other symptoms of disease. If some of the leaves are very badly marked, you may want to remove them. Spots, of themselves, will not kill a leaf.

Leaf spots may seem to disfigure a plant, but if you use them to more closely examine your treatment of your plants, and as an early warning system of disease, you may find that they are of some help to you in improving your gardening.

MILDEWS

Mildews are powdery, grey downy growths that coat leaf surfaces. Because mildews interfere with the vital process of photosynthesis, they can seriously affect a plant's health. Mildews appear in an excessively humid environment, where there is little ventilation.

A well ventilated greenhouse, in which the humidity is sufficient, but not excessive, should have few attacks of mildew. If an occasional plant should develop mildew, remove badly affected leaves and treat the rest of the plant with a spray of Karathane (two teaspoons to a gallon of water).

MOLDS

Molds are rapidly proliferating fungus infections. Fortunately, only two types of mold commonly occur on plants.

A sooty black mold covering portions of leaves is a sign of an aphid, mealybug or scale infestation. While the mold does not greatly harm leaves, it does attract ants. If a sooty mold is severe it may interfere with the plant's photosynthesizing. It is also unattractive.

A pale white or grayish mold appearing on the soil surface is a sign of overwatering. It can grow only in soil that is constantly damp — and most of your plants don't require continuously damp soil. Soil that is always wet can encourage the spread of rot, or attact other infections.

Gently wash off sooty molds with lukewarm soapy water. Scrape the gray mold off the soil surface, or thoroughly turn the soil and mix the mold in. Cut back on your watering.

ROOT ROT

Root rot can be a fatal problem. Part of the trouble is that you may not be aware of its presence until serious damage has been done. Infected roots cannot draw in sufficient moisture and nourishment to keep a plant alive, and the plant dies of either thirst or malnutrition.

A plant suffering from root rot may have leaves that brown, wilt and fall off. The stem of the plant may become entirely bare for a substantial part of the plant's height. And although the plant may appear badly in need of water, you will find that no amount of water will be of any help.

If you suspect root rot, turn a plant out of its pot, or remove it from the bench in which it is rooted. Clear all soil away from the roots, and examine them thoroughly. Shriveled, discolored or pulpy roots indicate rot. Pare the roots back to the healthy root growth with a knife, and dust the new ends with a fungicide. After you are satisfied that you have removed all the root rot, re-pot the plant in fresh soil. For the first week, water the plant sparingly. If a plant rooted in a bench develops rot, you may have to remove and examine all of the plants surrounding it. And if any other plants in the bench develop rot, I suggest that you empty the bench, discard the soil and replace it with fresh, sterilized soil.

TREATING PESTS AND DISEASES WITH CHEMICALS

You will often have to use some chemical preparation to treat an infested or infected plant.

Never use a stronger preparation than you have to.

Apply a preparation only to treat a specific insect or infection, or to protect a plant from a possible specific problem.

And when you apply a preparation, read all of the instructions for use and follow them to the letter.

Never handle chemicals in a confined or unventilated area. Try not to breathe in the fumes. If you are working with a liquid, be careful not to splash any on your skin or clothes. If you do, wash the area immediately with soap and water.

After treating a plant, keep it away from children or animals.

If you spray a plant, spray it only in a well ventilated place.

If you are working with a liquid preparation — something that you must dilute in water — make only as much as you estimate you will need. If there is any remaining solution, discard it.

Store all of the chemicals you keep on hand in tight containers, on a shelf high enough to discourage prying hands. Or store them in a cabinet that you can then lock. If any of the preparations are aerosol sprays, store them away from heat and sunlight.

What kinds of pesticides are available?

There are contact poisons, that kill on contact soon after they are applied to a plant.

There are stomach poisons, that are applied to the foliage. When the pest eats the foliage, it dies.

There are systemics, which are applied to an infested plant's soil. The poison is drawn up through the roots, as it is suspended in water, and distributed through all of the plant. The entire plant becomes poison bait — wherever a bug takes a bite, it will be swallowing poison. Systemics will go on working for several weeks in a plant.

Drenches are liquid solutions applied to the soil, as opposed to solutions sprayed on the foliage. While most drenches are contact posions, meant to kill bugs in the soil, some also kill bugs in a foliage as their vapors dissipate upwards.

Malathion is the name of a contact pesticide. It can be mixed in water and sprayed on a plant's foliage or applied to its soil. It can kill many of the commonest of plant pests. I have stressed its use because it is relatively non-toxic to mammals. However, it will not kill all types of bugs, and it can be harmful to some kinds of plants, such as ferns. The label will tell you which plants and bugs it can be used on.

Fungicides are contact poisons. They can be purchased as liquids, or powders that must be dissolved in liquids, and they are used to end a disease.
Bordeaux mixture, Captan, Ferbam and Maneb are all fungicides.

Miticides are contact insecticides intended for use against spider mites. They should not be used on edible plants. Dimite and Tedion are miticides.

Nicotine Sulfate can be sprayed on foliage or applied to the soil to control some types of insects. As it can be quite toxic, be especially careful not to inhale any vapors as you work with this poison.

Rotenone is a contact insecticide that is used to control a number of types of insects. It is an organic substance, made from the leaves of a plant, and is said to be one of the safest of the pesticides as it is non-toxic to mammals.

Ced-O-Flora is a liquid composed of petroleum products, soap and oils. It is used to treat scale and mealybug attacks.

Systemics are available as liquid concentrates or powders. While they are lethally effective, I can recommend them for only the stubbornest of infestations. They turn an entire plant into poison bait, and they linger on. The chance of an accident, such as a child or animal chewing a leaf plucked from the plant, is too great for me to consider using systemics except in severe infestations. If you must use it, then by all means don't hesitate. But remember that there are other, less dangerous preparations, and only when you are faced by a very bad problem should anything so toxic as a systemic be used.

How are these preparations applied to a plant?

Many kinds of poisons are available as liquid concentrates, and can be used as either a spray or a drench for the soil. To use as a spray, dilute a preparation with water according to the instructions on the package. Pour the liquid into a hand-held sprayer, and apply an abundant mist to plant leaves or leaf axils, and to the underside of leaves, as they frequently serve as a hiding place for pests.

A drench is prepared from a liquid concentrate or a powder dissolved in water. You can use a watering can to apply a drench to a plant's soil. You might want to keep a small watering can for just such use, to be sure that no pesticides end up in your regular plant water supply.

Aerosol sprays are the most inexact, and often the weakest, of treatments. I do not recommend them. Nor do I recommend the use of other pesticides that do not specifically state that they can be safely used around plants. Some gardeners bring pest strips, traps, baits and other pest control devices into their greenhouses. I do not. Cleanliness and vigilance will give you as much protection as they can, and they present no risk. The vapors from some poisons can harm plants. And, in a relatively small working area, repeated exposure could even harm you.

When you must use chemicals to end an infestation:

Read all of the instructions on each package. Be certain to which plants the preparation can be safely applied, and exactly how to apply it.

Unless you have a very serious infestation that threatens to spread throughout the unit, use the mildest of all the poisons applicable to your problem.

Do not inhale the fumes of any of these preparations.

If you spill or accidentally spray any of these chemicals on yourself, wash it off with hot soapy water immediately.

Keep all chemicals sealed and away from children.

When you use them, apply the recommended dosage and **no more**.

Never use poisons when there are non-chemical means of control that will work as efficently to end an infestation.

Poisons are one of several techniques for preventing or ending insect attacks. Some infestations can be ended by scrubbing a plant with soapy water. Other non-chemical methods have proved equally effective in ending infestations. Many of these methods have been mentioned in this chapter, and I would like to encourage you to try them, or to invent others for your own use.

Chemicals should be your last — not your first — line of defense in the greenhouse. You will certainly need them, and it is always better to use them then to lose any plants. But please don't reach for the poison at the first sign of trouble. Identify the problem, and match the treatment to the trouble.

When you must use chemicals, use them on specific plants. Unless your entire unit is infested, I strongly suggest that you treat one plant at a time. While some commercial growers do seal and fumigate an entire greenhouse to rid it of pests, this procedure cannot be recommended for the home gardener. You really shouldn't have any trouble that bad. And by blanketing ill and healthy plants alike, you always take the chance of increasing, rather than decreasing your plant losses.

Chemicals are an increasingly important part of insect control — but they are not wonder workers. They cannot remedy all of the problems you might face. They cannot keep a greenhouse clean or in order — only you can do that. Chemicals are a tool, and one that you must use wisely if you are to use it well.

Chapter 14

PROFITS?

Most greenhouse gardeners aren't in it for the money. The pleasure they derive from working in their units, they would say, is a sufficient return on their investment.

If they investigate their neighborhood they will discover that a tremendous demand exists for all kinds of green life. Plant shops, a relatively recent arrival, now number in the thousands all across the country. Florists are carrying more flowering and foliage plants because they have encountered a greatly increased need. Other outlets, such as department and discount stores, also report a much greater volume of business in plants. Plants have become big business, but it has happened so fast that demand often exceeds supply. And that means the opportunities may exist in your area for a small supplier.

If you are considering growing plants for profit, there are several things you must do. You must take a survey of the local market — who sells plants in your area? You might approach some of the people that do, suggest the idea and find out if they would be interested. However, no one is going to give you a definite answer unless you demonstrate that you can deliver. Take a long and critical look at your abilities and the capacities of your unit. It is one thing to occasionally present a friend with an especially attractive African Violet, but it is quite different to sign a contract where you agree to supply twenty African Violets with

some regularity. If you don't have the experience, or if your unit isn't big enough to handle such production, don't even attempt it.

There is an even more important question that must be resolved before you begin: are you certain that you want to do it? Keep in mind that gardening for money is quite different from gardening for pleasure — you will have deadlines to meet, and your contract will call for a specific number of plants of a certain quality. Fulfilling your part of an agreement is going to take time, disciplined effort and vigilance, because you literally cannot afford to have anything go wrong. While you are laboring to meet your commitment, all the pleasure of leisurely gardening may fly out the greenhouse sash. If your gardening affords you relaxation and satisfaction, you would probably be well advised to be content with that. Don't turn your greenhouse into a dollars-and-cents operation unless you're just in it for the money.

You can produce a variety of items for sale, including flowering and foliage plants, cut flowers, or seeds. Some gardeners buy the materials necessary for making corsages, and turn out quantities of corsages when there is a demand for them. Of course, you can also use your imagination to come up with some other saleable product or service. For instance, I know of one greenhouse gardener who began offering gardening classes for children in his unit.

He was so successful that he added classes for adults. He is retired, and the classes bring in some extra income, while affording him the pleasure of introducing others to the satisfactions of gardening.

Before you go into business, take a careful accounting to determine what your expenses will be, and how much you will have to charge to make a profit. After investing considerable time and effort in a project, it would be frustrating to do no more than break even because you had miscalculated your expenses.

Your greenhouse might have the potential to help you increase your income — **if** it is large enough, **if** you have the experience to raise large, uniform crops of plants, and **if** you can devote sufficient time to the work.

Do it if you have to. Or do it because you enjoy the challenge of growing and selling crops of plants. But don't do it if you consider your greenhouse primarily a source of quiet, unhurried pleasures. If you garden to escape the pressure of the world, I suggest you leave all thoughts of business outside your greenhouse door.

SOURCES

GREENHOUSE MANUFACTURERS

Aluminum Greenhouse Inc.
14615 Lorain Avenue
Cleveland, Ohio 44111

Units begin at $250

American-Moniger Greenhouse Manufacturing Co.
1820 Flushing Avenue
Brooklyn, New York 11237

W. Atlee Burpee Company
5275 Burpee Building
Warminster, Pennsylvania 18974

The Burpee "English Greenhouse"
is priced slightly under $600

Enclosures Inc.
80 Main Street
Moreland, Georgia 30259

Units costing several hundred
dollars, and up

Environmental Dynamics
3010-CE Vine Street
Sunnymead, California 92507

Units priced from $90

Gothic Arch Greenhouses
Department 1-3
Post Office Box 1564
Mobile, Alabama 36601

Units costing "about $2.50
per square foot"

Janco Greenhouses
Box 348
10788 Tucker Street
Department H-3
Beltsville, Maryland 20705

Lord and Burnham
Irvington-on-Hudson
New York 10533

Units priced from $195
up to $2,500

McGregor Greenhouses
Box 36-5F
Santa Cruz, California 95063

Peter Reimuller
P.O. Box 2666-A5
Santa Cruz, California 95063

Units priced from $120

Redferns Pre-Fab Greenhouse Manufacturing Co.
3842 Scott's Valley Drive
Santa Cruz, California 95060

Redwood Domes
Aptos, California 95003

Units priced from $100

Stearns Greenhouses
98 Taylor Street
Neponset, Massachusetts 02122

Sturdi-Built Manufacturing Co.
11304 S.W. Boone's Ferry Road
Portland, Oregon 97219

Sunshine Greenhouses
Box 3577
Torrance, California 90510

Units priced from $100

Texas Greenhouse Company, Inc.
2709 St. Louis Avenue
Ft. Worth, Texas 76110

Turner Greenhouses
Route 117
Goldsboro, North Carolina 27530

Vegetable Factory Greenhouses
P.O. Box 2235
Department H-3
Grand Central Station
New York City, New York 10017

Units priced from $500

Most of the manufacturers listed offer a variety of greenhouse sizes and designs. All of them will send material describing their products and listing costs upon request.

Many of them also carry greenhouse accessories, such as heaters, fans, thermometers, humidifiers etc. — so even if you are not shopping for a pre-fab greenhouse, you should be able to purchase from manufacturers many of the accessories you will need.

GREENHOUSE PLANS

Environment
Box 7855
Austin, Texas 78712

Offers an illustrated booklet of two greenhouse construction plans for $2.00

Greenhouse Specialties
9849-H Kimker
St. Louis, Missouri 63127

Plans for fiberglass greenhouses, along with prices for materials and accessories, for $1.00

Liahona Greenhouses
Box 17060
Salt Lake City, Utah 48117

Plans for three greenhouses, for $2.00

Werth's
Box 1902GD
Cedar Rapids, Iowa 52406

5 Plans for greenhouses for $2.00

Your state Agricultural Extension Service, or your county Agricultural agent, should be able to furnish a plan for constructing your own greenhouse.

SOURCES FOR SEEDS AND PLANTS

Abbey Garden
Box 167
Reseda, California 91335
succulents

Abbots Nursery
Route 4, Box 482
Mobile, Alabama 36609

Alberts & Merkel Brothers
P.O. Box 537
Boynton Beach, Florida 33435
orchids, tropical foliage plants.

Black River Orchids, Inc.
P.O. Box 110
Dept. H.
S. Haven, Michigan 49090
orchids

Buell's Greenhouses
Eastford, Connecticut 06242
gesneriads

Burgess Seed and Plant Company
P.O. Box 218
Galesburg, Michigan 49053
seeds and plants

Edelweiss Gardens
Robbinsville, New Jersey 08691
plants

Farmer Seed and Nursery Company
Faribault, Minnesota 55021

Fennell Orchid Company
26715 Southwest 157th Avenue
Homestead, Florida 33030
orchids

Fischer Greenhouse
Linwood, New Jersey 08221
African violets

Joseph Harris Co., Inc.
Moreton Farm, Buffalo Road
Rochester, New York 14624
vegetable seeds

Alexander I. Heimlich 71 Burlington Street Woburn, Massachusetts 01801	bulbs, tubers and corms
Margaret Ilgenfritz P.O. Box 665 Monroe, Michigan 48161	orchids
Michael J. Kartuz 92 Chestnut Street Wilmington, Massachusetts 91887	plants
Lyndon Lyon Dolgeville, New York 13329	African violets
Rod McClellan Company 1450 El Camino Real S. San Francisco, California 94080	orchids
Merry Gardens Camden, Maine 04843	plants
McComb Greenhouses New Straitsville, Ohio 43766	ferns, cacti, house plants
Nature's Garden Route 1, Box 488 Beaverton, Oregon 97005	wildflowers, rock plants
Pearce Seed Company Moorestown, New Jersey 08057	
Reasoner's Tropical Nurseries, Inc. P.O. Box 1881 Bradenton, Florida	
Clyde Robin P.O. Box 2855 Castro Valley, California 94546	wildflowers, herbs, vegetables $1 for the catalog
John Scheepers, Inc. 37 Wall Street New York City, New York 10005	bulbs
Stern's Nurseries, Inc. Geneva, New York 14456	

Sun Dew Environments P.O. Box 503 Boston, Massachusetts 02115	Carnivorous plants
Thon's Mums 4815 Oak Crystal Lake, Illinois 60014	Chrysanthemums
Tinari Greenhouses Box 190 2325 Valley Road Huntingdon Valley, Pennsylvania 19006	African violets
Van Sciver's Dutch Gardens Pocono Mountains, Box 12 Tannersville, Pennsylvania 18372	Tuberous begonias
Velco Importers 3171 Purdue Avenue Los Angeles, California 90066	Bromeliads
Volkmann Brothers Greenhouses 2714 Minert Street Dallas, Texas 75219	African violets
Westover Greenhouse 1317 N. 175th Street Seattle, Washington 98133	Fuchsias
White Flower Farm Esther's Lane Litchfield, Connecticut 06759	Begonias, delphiniums
Wilson Brothers Roachdale, Indiana 46172	Geraniums

This is only a sample of the suppliers marketing products through the mail. **The Gardener's Catalogue** (Tom Riker and Harvey Rottenberg, William Morrow and Company, 1974) has extensive lists of suppliers for all types of plants and seeds. In addition, many horticultural publications carry ads placed by suppliers. **Horticulture** magazine, for instance, published monthly by the Massachusetts Horticulture Society, carries an extensive and informative section of advertisements. If at all possible, I suggest that you check for what you need at local garden centers or nurseries, so that you may avoid having to wait for materials to arrive through the mails.

INDOOR LIGHTING SUPPLIES

Armstrong Associates, Inc.
Box 127 BK
Basking Ridge, New Jerse 07920

California Crafts
Box 2342-H3
Santa Cruz, California 95063

Plans for building inexpensive indoor light gardens, $2.00

Floralite
4124 H
East Oakwood Road
Oak Creek, Wisconsin 53154

Variety of Gro-lites and tubes, including Starlite garden lamps, Spot-o-Sun, Vita-lite and Naturescent tubes.

House Plant Corner
Box 165-S
Oxford, Maryland 21654

25¢ for a catalogue including selections of soils and lights.

Lifelite Incorporated
1025 Shary Circle
Concord, California 94520

Rapid Lite
245 South Broadway
Yonkers, New York 10705

Shoplite Company
566 J Franklin Avenue
Nutley, New Jersey 07110

The Indoor Light Gardening Society of America, Inc.
Department H
128 West 58th Street
New York City, New York 10019

The Society publishes a bi-monthly magazine, and is an excellent source of information on many aspects of gardening with lights. Membership dues $5.00.

CANADIAN SOURCES

Atlas Asbestos Company
5600 Hochelaga Street
Montreal, H1N 1W1

Greenhouse panels, composed
of fiberglass

Canadian Greenhouses, Inc.
P.O. Box 5000
Durham Road
Beamsville, Ontario L0R 1B0

Variety of pre-fab greenhouses

Ickes-Braun Glasshouses of Canada Ltd.
P.O. Box 2000
90 Bartlett Road
Beamsville, Ontario L0R 1B0

Steel and fiberglass
greenhouses

Lord & Burnham Company Limited
325 Welland Avenue
St. Catharines, Ontario

Greenhouses and greenhouse
accessories

Glen D. Ogilivie Limited
Box 329
Caledonia, Ontario

Greenhouses

Outland-Hafco Ltd.
55 Glen Cameron Road
Thornhill, Ontario

P.V.C. greenhouses and accessories

SUPPLIES

Canadian Industries Limited
Lawn and Garden Products Department
P.O. Box 5201
London, Ontario N6A 4L6

Fertilizers, manures
and insecticides

Chevron Chemical Limited (Ortho Division)
1060 Industry Street
Oakville, Ontario

Fertilizers

Chipman Chemicals Limited
Hamilton, Ontario

Pesticides

GTE Sylvania Canada Ltd.
8750 Cote deLiesse Road
Montreal, Quebec H4T 1H3

Complete Line of lighting
products for home and
greenhouse gardening

National Garden Supply of Canada Ltd.
150 Duke Street
Bowmanville, Ontario

Wide variety of gardening supplies, including fertilizers, pesticides, manures, tools

United Co-Operatives of Canada
2549 Weston Road
Weston Ontario

Fertilizers, pesticides, seed, gardening tools

Some of these firms may not conduct business through the mails, but they can refer you to outlets in your area, and many of them offer descriptive materials.

BIBLIOGRAPHY

Blake, Claire: **Greenhouse Gardening for Fun.** New York, William Morrow and Company, 1972.

Chabot, Ernest: **The New Greenhouse Gardening for Everyone.** New York, Barrows, 1955.

Crockett, James U.: **Greenhouse Gardening as a Hobby.** Garden City, New York, Doubleday and Company, 1961.

- - - - - - - - - - - - (ed.): **Greenhouse Handbook for the Amateur.** Brooklyn, New York, The Brooklyn Botanic Gardens, 1971.

Eaton, Jerome A.: **Gardening Under Glass.** New York, Macmillan, 1973.

Faust, Joan Lee: **New York Times Book of House Plants.** New York, A&W Publishing, 1975.

Free, Montague: **Plant Propagation in Pictures.** Garden City, Doubleday, 1957.

Haring, Elda: **Complete Book of Growing Plants from Seed.** New York, Hawthorn, 1967.

Kramer, Jack: **Grow Your Own Plants.** New York, Charles Scribner's Sons, 1973.

Kranz, Frederick H. and Jacqueline L.: **Gardening Indoors Under Lights.** New York, Viking, 1971.

McDonald, Elvin: **Handbook for Greenhouse Gardeners.** Irvington-on-Hudson, New York, Lord & Burnham, 1971.

Markel, J.L. & Noble, Mary: **Gardening in a Small Greenhouse.** New York, D. Van Nostrand Company, 1956.

Nicholls, Richard: **The Plant Doctor.** Philadelphia, Running Press, 1975.

Northern, Henry T.: **Greenhouse Gardening.** New York, Ronald Press, 1973.

Potter, Charles H.: **Greenhouse: Place of Magic.** New York, E.P. Dutton & Company, 1967.

Preston, F.G.: Greenhouse: **A Complete Guide to the Construction and Management of Greenhouses of All Kinds.** New York, Taplinger Publishing Company, 1958.

Taylor, Kathryn S. and Gregg, Edith W.: **Winter Flowers in Greenhouse and Sun-Heated Pit.** New York, Scribner's Sons, 1969.

Taylor, Norman (ed.): **Taylor's Encyclopedia of Gardening.** Boston, Houghton Mifflin, 1961.

Westcott, Cynthia: **The Gardener's Bug Book.** Garden City, New York, Doubleday, 1973.

BOOKS ON TOOLS AND BUILDING TECHNIQUES

Better Homes and Gardens Handyman's Book: New York, Bantam, 1970.

Campbell, Robert: **How to Work with Tools and Wood,** New York, Pocket Books, 1974.

Day Richard: **The Home Owner Handbook of Plumbing and Heating,** New York, Bounty Books, 1974.

Reader's Digest Complete Do-It-Yourself Manual, Pleasantville, New York, Reader's Digest, 1973.
Sunset Books: Menlo Park, California

   Basic Carpentry Illustrated
   Garden and Patio Building Book
   Garden Work Centers.

The Superintendent of Documents, U.S. Government Printing Office, Washington, D.C. 20402 offers a wide variety of inexpensive bookets on building techniques and on buying and using materials.

INDEX